applied anthropology

applied anthropology

GEORGE M. FOSTER
University of California, Berkeley

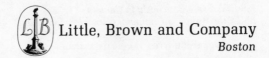 Little, Brown and Company
Boston

FIRST PRINTING

Published simultaneously in Canada
by Little, Brown & Company (Canada) Limited

PRINTED IN THE UNITED STATES OF AMERICA

preface

When anthropologists utilize their theoretical concepts, factual knowledge, and research methodologies in programs meant to ameliorate contemporary social, economic, and technological problems, they are engaging in applied anthropology. This is a specialized subdiscipline within the broad field of anthropology, in which traditional interests have been theoretical rather than practical and in which most time and effort are devoted to university teaching and university-based research. The practical problems to which anthropologists have turned their attention have varied over the years. During the first part of this century the administration of dependent peoples was the primary interest of applied anthropology. With the end of the colonial system after World War II, applied anthropological interest has shifted to the social and cultural problems that accompany technological change and modernization in both industrialized and developing countries. Today applied anthropologists are primarily concerned with processes of social and cultural change, particularly as they bear upon planned improvements in such fields as agriculture, health and medical services, educational systems, social welfare programs, community development, and the like.

Authors of books about applied anthropology have approached the topic from a variety of points of view. Some have described and analyzed cases of technical and social change in which anthropologists have participated as specialists in human relations. This approach has been used successfully in a number of case-books, including Spicer, *Human Problems in Technological Change* (1952), Paul, *Health, Culture and Community* (1955), and Barnett, *Anthropology in Administration* (1956). Others have concentrated on social and economic change, as they have been studied by anthropologists working on problems of development and modernization. This point of view is well documented in recent volumes such as Erasmus, *Man Takes Control* (1961), Foster, *Traditional Cultures: and the Impact of Technological Change* (1962), Goodenough, *Cooperation in Change* (1963), and Arensberg and Niehoff, *Technical Cooperation and Cultural Reality* (1963). Still other authors have illustrated problems and methods by concentrating on specific fields, such as Spindler, *Education and Culture* (1963). Batten, *The Human Factor in Community Work* (1965), and Read, *Culture, Health, and Disease* (1966).

In this book, I approach the topic from a point of view heretofore little explored in anthropology: that of the basic relationship between theoretical and applied science. Within this context, anthropology is considered as a special case of a general class of phenomena. I take it for granted that applied anthropology deals largely with social and cultural change, particularly of the kind encountered in the development and modernization of the contemporary world. Chapter 1 contains examples of some of these change problems to which applied research lends itself, as well as several summaries of case studies in which anthropologists played major roles in facilitating change. In Chapter 2, I take up the

problem of defining applied anthropology, and describe a model
which relates scientific and action-oriented activities to the personnel involved at the several stages in the discovery-to-utilization
sequence of the scientific endeavor. I suggest that what makes
anthropology "applied" is not the research itself, nor special training of the anthropologist, but rather the kind of relationship he
enjoys with an innovating organization. When this organization
determines the general area of research, sponsors it, has propri-
etary rights to the research results, and uses them in its planning
and operations, then an anthropologist is doing applied work.

In Chapter 3, this question is asked: "What is there in the science of anthropology that is pertinent to the search for solutions
to contemporary social change problems?" I find the answer to be
not so much general theory which can be "applied" to practical
problems, as a remarkably flexible and adaptable research methodology, exploratory in nature, which enhances the likelihood of
discovering the significant social and cultural problems in directed change programs. This methodology, and especially the
assumptions that underlie it, are discussed at some length. Chapters 4 through 6 pinpoint and examine the three principal foci
toward which this research methodology is directed in applied
work: the target or client group which is the object of concern to
an innovating organization; the structure and values of the innovating organization itself; and the setting in which these two
"systems" come together.

As in other scientific fields, the kind of work an anthropologist
does has a good deal to do with his professional status. Applied
anthropology enjoys less prestige than does theoretically oriented
anthropology. In Chapter 7, I examine the reasons for this relative
lack of status, and suggest that a common misconception about
the relationships between theoretical and applied social science
research contributes to this state of affairs. Chapter 8 deals with
the problem of administrative ties between anthropologists and
operations personnel—the planners, administrators, and technical experts of directed change programs—which frequently have
been marked by friction, neither group being entirely satisfied

with the relationship. The reasons for this comparative lack of satisfaction, I argue, are due to the differing goals and forms of ego gratification characterizing the two groups.

In anthropology, as in society at large, the present is best understood only when viewed against the past. Applied anthropology has a history stretching back for more than half a century, and knowledge of this history helps us to understand the field as it is today, its evaluation by the profession, the handicaps under which it labors, and its potential for the future. In Chapter 9, the origins and development of applied anthropology are sketched.

Applied Anthropology deals only with the work of social anthropologists, neglecting several important subfields of the science. Applied archaeology, such as that used in reconstructing Williamsburg, Virginia, and Fort Ross, California, is ignored, as are applied physical anthropology and applied linguistics (which has led to vastly improved methods for teaching foreign languages). With much less justification, applied anthropology in industry is not considered. This highly specialized field is best treated, it seems to me, as a separate topic.

The data and ideas in *Applied Anthropology* have a tripartite origin: more than a generation of research on social and cultural change processes; fifteen years' experience with students in graduate and undergraduate applied anthropology courses, especially in public health and community development; and assignments as consultant, adviser, and evaluator in technical development programs in many parts of the world. I have carried out basic research in Mexico and Spain, particularly in the mestizo, Spanish-speaking peasant village of Tzintzuntzan, Michoacán, Mexico, which I have studied since 1944 and from which I draw numerous examples (Foster 1948, 1967a). As Lecturer in Public Health I gave a graduate seminar in anthropology and health for several years in the School of Public Health at the University of California, Berkeley. Annually since 1958, an interdisciplinary faculty group at the University, under contract with the Agency for International Development, has offered to foreign and American specialists a semester-long seminar on community development. I have played an active role in these seminars, in which nationals of more than thirty countries have participated. In addition, each fall I give an Upper Division course called "Anthropology in Modern Life." These varied teaching experiences have been invaluable in shaping my thinking about the role of the anthropologist in contemporary life.

In 1951–1952, while employed by the Smithsonian Institution, my anthropological colleagues and I participated in a major evaluation of the first decade of American bilateral cooperative health programs in Latin America, research sponsored by the Institute of Inter-American Affairs and the United States Public Health Service. The American foreign aid program, currently called the Agency for International Development, sent me as consultant in community development to India, Pakistan, and the Philippines in 1955, to Afghanistan in 1957, to Northern Rhodesia (now Zambia) in 1961 and 1962, and to Nepal in 1965. The Organization of American States gave me similar, short-term assignments in Mexico and Bolivia in 1963 and 1964. In 1952 I served as adviser to the American delegation to the Fifth World Health Assembly in Geneva, and in 1966 I participated in the Third World Congress of Medical Education in New Delhi.

The people who made these rich experiences possible are Mr. Louis Miniclier, Mrs. Barbara Doyle, Dr. John Cool, Dr. Henry Van Zile Hyde, and Dr. Gabriel Ospina. I wish here publicly to acknowledge my appreciation to these friends, as well as to the many people, members of American missions and nationals of the countries in which I worked, who became my close friends in the course of these assignments. Dwight Heath, Margaret Lantis, and Kalervo Oberg read the first draft of this book and made many helpful suggestions which are incorporated in the final version. I am particularly indebted to Susan Currier for her careful analysis of the manuscript, and for judicious advice on matters of content and style, and to her husband, Richard, whose insights have significantly aided me on points of organization.

GEORGE M. FOSTER

contents

applied anthropology

CHAPTER 1   the nature of
                                applied anthropology

AN EXAMPLE OF THE PROBLEM

For many years the Mexican Ministry of Health has carried out major environmental sanitation work in rural areas. Projects include village potable water supply systems, sanitary latrines, shower baths with hot water, and batteries of centrally located washtubs, which make it unnecessary for village women to carry laundry to streams where they wash under uncomfortable conditions in cold water. A Ministry engineer designed and built a combination bath house and washtub unit in a small community in the State of Veracruz. To conserve materials and space he followed the sound engineering practice of putting a single row of tubs against the back wall of the building that contained shower baths. To his surprise, village women, far from being grateful for the new convenience, chided him: "Ay, engineer, why are you punishing us?," they asked. Astonished, he asked how he was punishing them. They replied that when a child in school misbehaves he is made to stand face to wall, and that is the way they felt with the new washtubs, which forced them to face the back wall of the shower building. Actually, of course, they were telling him that work is lighter when the position of the workers encourages conversation and gossip and laughter. Because of these complaints, and the reluctance of the women to use the new tubs, the engineer changed the design so that a long arm of pairs of washtubs projected at right angles from the rear of the shower house. With the new construction the women faced each other across their tubs and, since the design encouraged social interaction, they happily accepted the innovation (communicated by Héctor García Manzanedo).

This incident illustrates what, in the literature on development and modernization, is called "planned" or "directed" culture change. It also illustrates how something that appears at first glance to be a simple technological problem in design is in fact equally a social problem. Only when the social imperatives as well as the technological objectives of the project were met could it be considered a success. In a sense, of course, all change can be called "planned," since any individual who innovates is engaged in personal planning and decision making, even if the event represents only a whim of the moment. A Mexican farmer who visits a friend in another village, notices that he is using chemical fertilizer, asks about its use, its cost, where it can be obtained, and then returns home and applies some to his field, is engaged in planned change. But the decision is individual, and not the consequence of major group planning and action.

The words "directed" and "planned" change today have come to have a special meaning: government, international, and private organizations are created in response to what are recognized as collective problems or needs of society. They are budgeted and are staffed with the planners, administrators, scientists, and technical specialists needed to achieve the goals that, it is hoped, will alleviate the problems that brought the organizations into being. City, county, and state public health departments are instruments of directed culture change programs, since through planning and action they are modifying prevailing health practices and behavior in the direction of longer life and less illness. County agricultural extension agents direct culture change by communicating improved farming practices and knowledge to the farmers of their districts. United States government foreign aid educators are agents of directed culture change, since they analyze traditional educational systems and, working with counterparts in host countries, plan and establish improved educational systems more nearly consonant with the needs of contemporary life.

THE TWO SIDES OF
DIRECTED CULTURE CHANGE

Directed culture change goals are dual, almost always involving changes both in the physical environment and in the behavior of people. In the example with which we began, the design and construction of the shower house and washtubs is a change in environment, while the utilization of showers and washtubs is a change in behavior. Environmental modification, which means design and construction, is often looked upon as the heart of national development and modernization, and the achievement of physical goals symbolizes the successful completion of each project. Yet if the appropriate changes in behavior do not accompany environmental modification, a project is of dubious merit. Listing X washtubs completed by a health ministry in its annual budget request may look impressive, but unless the tubs are used — that is, unless there is a corresponding change in the behavior of washerwomen — the accomplishment is of no value.

During the several decades in which massive planned culture change on a worldwide scale has been recognized as essential to raising standards of living, there has been a strong tendency to assume that design and construction that meet the highest standards of the profession or professions involved in a project is the primary goal of development. It is assumed that successful environmental modification through sound design and engineering will automatically engender changes in behavior. In other words, if people are presented with what planners and designers feel to be better ways of doing things, they will be eager to accept the innovations.

Experience shows that this is not necessarily so. There seem to be two basic reasons why people, when presented with "improved" environments or opportunities, do not rush to avail themselves of the benefits of the innovation:

1. The innovation, in the total life context of the community, is not in fact an improvement. It is better called a "pseudo-improvement," since its social and other costs outweigh its advantages.

2. The innovation may by all reasonable standards be well planned and represent a genuine improvement, but the people for whom it is intended may not perceive the advantages, or they may be reluctant to try it because of cultural, social, and psychological barriers that discourage innovation. We will consider the implications of each of these reasons in turn.

RESISTANCE TO PSEUDO-IMPROVEMENTS

Planning and design for improvements in directed change programs are executed by members of the several professions: architects, engineers, city and regional planners, agricultural and irrigation specialists, public health physicians and nurses, educators, and many others. Almost always they define "problems" within their narrow professional frameworks, and they seek answers within the same context. To illustrate, improved agricultural practices that will result in higher crop yields from a given area are rightly seen as a major step forward in the fight against hunger, other factors being equal. But other factors are not always equal. In Nepal, foreign agricultural specialists pursuing this goal introduced a Japanese rice that, with the associated cultivation techniques, produced up to 200 per cent more crop than the native rice. Narrowly defined, this was a great achievement. But the Japanese rice proved unpopular for two reasons. It grows on a dwarf stalk that provides much less fodder than the indigenous rice, and since animal fodder is a major by-product from rice cultivation, failure to provide sufficient fodder produced an animal feed crisis. Moreover, the seeds cling tightly to the stalks, necessitating a special threshing machine not normally available to farmers. So, in the total context of the Nepalese farmers' needs and possibilities, an "improved" practice was of doubtful value (author's field notes).

"Improved" design as seen by the professional is not necessarily improved design as seen by the potential user. The best solution to a specific need is not a professional absolute, capable of application anywhere in the world. Rather, the appropriate answer is a function of local cultural, social, and economic forms, one element in a complex of related factors. If "improved" designs or recommended practices do serious violence to any of the social, cultural, or psychological needs and expectations of the people involved, they probably will be rejected. These expectations and needs are not necessarily obvious, as countless failures in technical aid programs testify. Often they must be ferreted out by research and analysis. Then, when they are understood, the plan most likely to achieve project goals, and meet local needs, can be designed and excuted. The following three cases illustrate how "improved" design and practices failed to consider the total context in which they functioned. In the first illustration there is no reasonable answer; in fact, the "problem" seen by the planners did not exist. In the other two, when the barriers preventing acceptance were discovered, modifications in design and operations produced acceptance.

Cooking Stoves in Northern Rhodesia. Before Northern Rhodesia became the independent country of Zambia in 1964, its Ministry of Native Affairs was charged with community development projects in rural areas. Housing improvements, including more sanitary cooking facilities, were a major goal of this work. To this end community development officers designed ingenious stoves made from discarded oil drums. A door was cut in the side for inserting wood, and smoke was drawn off through a flue passing through the kitchen roof. But the several variations of this design were greeted with little enthusiasm. The reason was quite simple. Traditionally, cooking is done outdoors on a slightly raised clay hearth a yard in diameter, on which three stones or baked clay cylinders are placed to support the cooking pot. The ends of long sticks and branches are brought together beneath the pot and are gradually pushed inward as they burn. This system permits excellent heat control and obviates the need to cut firewood to length. The community development design, on the other hand, requires great labor in cutting wood into many small pieces, and heat control never was satisfactorily worked out. Moreover, outdoor cooking permits women in neighboring compounds to talk with each other as they work, whereas indoor cooking, isolating a woman in her dark kitchen, destroys the social advantages of the traditional way. For the conditions of village life the traditional cooking system is technically superior and socially more acceptable than that envisaged by the planners (author's field notes).

Cooking Stoves in Egypt. A kitchen stove with a flue that projected through the roof was designed for a rural housing project in the Nile Delta. The architects, however, failed to consider the stove in the wider context of village life. In this part of Egypt, dry cotton stalks used in cooking are stored on house roofs after harvest, as a consequence of which several houses with the new stoves caught fire and burned when sparks from the flue ignited this tinder. One solution to the problem, of course, would be to devise a new fuel storage system. But this type of storage has important social as well as technical functions. First, a great pile of stalks brings prestige because it is proof of skillful farming and a good crop. Second, it advertises hospitality; a heaping roof is an open invitation to the farmer's friends to come and drink tea with him. Hence, alternate storage systems, however sound from a technical and economic standpoint, do not meet the social and psychological needs of the villagers. Only when an efficient spark arrester was designed were villagers willing to use the new stoves (communicated by Mostafa H. Sultan).

Powdered Milk in a Venezuelan Health Clinic. When the Venezuelan Ministry of Health and Social Welfare opened rural maternal and child health clinics, powdered milk was distributed free of charge to mothers who faithfully kept their pre- and postnatal appointments. The free milk was intended to increase clinic attendance and to better nourish mothers and children. Some months later clinic attendance had risen gratifyingly, but pregnancy complications and nutritional levels showed little improvement. A survey showed many mothers were exchanging the government milk in stores that would give them liquor and adult foods. A number of factors were found to be responsible for this unexpected situation:

(a) Some mothers, when asked why they didn't give the milk to their infants, asked, "Is the milk from my breast so bad that I must use this powder?" These mothers felt threatened because the milk program reflected on their ability to fulfill the role of mother by nursing their infants.

(b) Other mothers felt it unfair for only the youngest people in the house to benefit from government largess. By exchanging the milk for other things, everyone in the house, and especially the husband, got a share.

(c) No initial attention was given to demonstrating the easiest ways to mix powdered milk, and the ways in which it could be combined with other foods.

When the social and economic factors were understood, steps were taken to combat the practice of exchanging milk for other items. Nurses in the clinics were instructed to open the cans before distributing them, making it more difficult for mothers to exchange milk for other goods. Then they gave more careful demonstrations on mixing and using the milk, giving prizes to the mothers who were most dextrous and ingenious in this task. These steps significantly increased milk consumption and raised nutritional levels (communicated by J. M. Brito-Stelling).

RESISTANCE TO WELL PLANNED IMPROVEMENTS

Cooking stoves in Northern Rhodesia were not real improvements. Cooking stoves in Egypt and powdered milk distribution in Venezuela were potential improvements, not fully realized until major changes were made in original plans. In other instances innovations are well planned and are genuine improvements, in spite of which they are opposed by the people for whom they are intended. Vaccination against smallpox, for example, almost always has been resisted initially by peasant villagers and primitive tribesmen. Improved seeds, insecticides, and fertilizers are often incredibly difficult to introduce, even when it seems there are no serious social or economic costs. Until very recent years villagers in Latin America frequently have failed to take full advantage of schooling opportunities presented to them by their governments. The reasons for these resistances are varied and cannot be explored in detail here. Basically, we can say that *communication* and *perception* problems are involved, that people fail to perceive advantage, and perhaps perceive disadvantage, in adopting the new ways. For parents with no understanding of scientific preventive medicine, who may feel — as do Indian villagers — that smallpox is a visitation of a god, the child's minor discomfort following vaccination, resulting in a sleepless night for him and his parents, may outweigh the uncertain advantages of immunization. Or to the parents it may seem impious to try to counteract the will of a deity who sends illness.

In many directed culture change programs the failure of the innovators to appreciate the cognitive orientation — the way in which stimuli are interpreted — and the perceptive reactions of people toward whom programs are directed results in misinterpretation. The United States Foreign Aid Program makes use of a pair of clasped hands on a shield as its symbol of friendship. This symbol is painted on government vehicles, on all signs showing American participation — everywhere, in fact, where it can reasonably advertise the American presence. In several parts of the world communists exploit this symbol by saying that it shows how American imperialists "pull people into slavery." And in Thailand, a pair of disembodied hands is disquietingly suggestive of the spirit world (communicated by Herbert Phillips). In Rhodesia, European health educators combating tuberculosis worked out a wall poster with a crocodile, one of the most deadly threats to African life, assuming this would impress Africans with the seriousness of TB symptoms. African villagers concluded that crocodiles cause tuberculosis, further confirming their belief that they should at all costs be avoided (*The Northern News*, Ndola, Northern Rhodesia, Sept. 27, 1961).

In Indonesia, prior to independence, the Dutch agricultural service prepared posters to recruit farmers in overcrowded areas for resettlement. The pictures showed rich rice fields and an attractive landscape, with a farmer, his wife, and a big, healthy girl in the foreground. Farther back, much smaller due to perspective, was a boy. The farmers saw that the new lands were fine for girls, but very bad for boys, since their growth obviously was stunted (communicated by Egbert DeVries).

Sometimes technically sound innovations in full harmony with the possibilities of the local culture are rejected or not fully exploited because the changes in behavior involved have negative aspects which deprive people of things they want, or threaten their security. In a small Mexican town a woman of the upper classes decided for prestige reasons to install a flush toilet. Since the town had long had running water there were no serious technical problems. The toilet, however, was rarely used. The woman told an anthropologist she really preferred the old latrine, a six-holer which she called the "ice cream parlor," because its boxlike construction and seat covers reminded her of the old-fashioned rows of cans in drug stores. Why did she prefer her "ice cream parlor"? Her friends joined her a time or two a day, and they passed a pleasant social hour, talking and smoking cigarettes. In this provincial, narrow-minded town, many people disapproved of women smoking, and this was the only place they could enjoy communal cigarettes without fear of censure (communicated by Catalina Garate de García).

Extension workers in an Indian village, where women use open fields for bodily needs, encountered the same reason for resistance to bore-hole latrines. Trips to the fields gave occasion to meet and talk with friends not otherwise seen. For young women of high caste who are strictly confined to their homes, this social opportunity is particularly important (Luschinsky 1963:67).

A wide variety of barriers, which I have discussed in detail elsewhere (Foster 1962, Chapters 5–7), inhibits the adoption of new material forms and practices of undoubted benefit. Of these, perhaps the most powerful in emerging societies is the conflict between traditional social ties and the expectation that people will share with others, and the desire of new entrepreneurs and others who make economic progress to keep their new gains for themselves and their immediate families. Hollnsteiner illustrates this principle as it works in the Philippines, where a farmer often is willing to buy fertilizer and work harder than when he farms with traditional methods, because he recognizes the increased rice yields. But he also fears his increased income will produce increased demands for help from his relatives, which will be hard to deny. "The potential drain on hard-earned surplus actually deters many Filipinos from trying to produce more" (Hollnsteiner 1963:202).

The same conflict is found in contemporary Africa. Marwick cites the example of labor migrants who have developed the custom of returning to their home villages after dark. When asked why they do this, they reply that they fear their relatives' envy of their prosperity will result in witchcraft directed against them. "According to African canons of co-operation, they should distribute their wealth among their relatives; but, having chosen the path of European individualism, they do not, and they feel guilty and project their guilt into fears of those whom, by African standards, they have wronged" (Marwick 1956:492). Among the Tonga of southern Zambia there are a good many elders with sufficient money to build improved homes, but many are afraid to do so. They believe that they may be bewitched or even killed by members of their families who feel there will be less for them if the money is squandered on a house in which they do not share (communicated by Ernest Mulube).

ANTHROPOLOGISTS IN DIRECTED CULTURE CHANGE PROGRAMS

Technological development and modernization obviously are not simple processes, since they must be based on the happy marriage

of professional plan and design with the realities of human behavior. In directed culture change programs there are inevitably
"human factors," some apparent, others subtle, but all critical to
the success of a project. Today anthropologists and other behavioral scientists often are asked to participate in such programs by
helping to achieve a design that is harmonious with the basic cultural patterns of the group, by analyzing what happens when
innovations are presented to recipient peoples, and by evaluating
projects that have been completed, in order to work out guide
lines for future planning and program implementation.

Anthropologists who work on directed culture change programs
whose goals have to do with the social and economic problems of
contemporary life, rather than with descriptive data and basic
theory about culture and society, are referred to as "applied anthropologists," and their professional activities as "applied anthropology." Actually, as we will show, very few anthropologists engage full time in this type of activity to the exclusion of academic
and other, similar interests, so that the expression "applied anthropology" usually *describes a role* an anthropologist may take on
from time to time, rather than describing a separate breed of
scientist.

Although for more than half a century there have been professional anthropologists, at least some of whose activities are properly described as "applied," general professional recognition of the
field's importance has come slowly, and even today many anthropologists look upon applied assignments as second-class work.
Anthropology has been accepted as a science for about a century,
and during this time most anthropologists have been concerned
primarily with theoretical rather than practical problems. At first
they were interested almost exclusively in the origin and evolution
of man as a physical being, in the appearance and gradual development of culture, and in its spread over the globe. Primitive
peoples were the subject matter of traditional anthropology, and
anthropologists saw their task to be discovering and documenting,
in all their variety, the ways of life of preliterate man, and reconstructing historical connections between different groups, utilizing

archaeological, linguistic, and cultural data. Although early antropologists insisted their science was "practical" (pages 182–183), the fact is that these interests, and the ideas and data they produced, did not readily lend themselves to the solution of practical problems. Nor, except in colonial administration, were there organizations which recognized the possibilities of anthropological research and advice in their programs.

In recent years anthropologists have widened their field of inquiry and amplified the foci of their investigations to include, in addition to primitive peoples, the study of peasant communities, urban neighborhoods, minority ethnic groups in their own societies, and specialized "cultures" such as those of hospitals and businesses. Two significant conceptual developments have accompanied this trend. First, anthropological interests have become increasingly sociological, concerned with the structure and function of social systems rather than with the exhaustive cataloguing of all aspects of a single culture. Second, concern with origins and past history has taken second place to interest in the dynamic processes of social change. Some anthropologists, of course, continue with the reconstruction of unwritten history of primitive peoples, and with determining probable migration routes and previous contacts between tribes now separated. But in a rapidly evolving world, with rural-to-urban migrations going on before our eyes, with the diffusion of city ways to villages, with more changes in attitudes, beliefs, and customs in a decade than formerly occurred in a millennium, the majority of anthropologists concentrate on these processes of modernization, on what we call "cultural dynamics" or "dynamics of change."

Process, rather than history, is the way we view change today. Concern with process has made it imperative to draw increasingly on the theory of other behavioral sciences, especially sociology and social psychology, so that anthropologists now work with such concepts as cognition, perception, motivation, social classes, social networks, and role relationships, as well as with more traditional concepts such as cultural patterns and cultural integration.

Contemporary anthropological interests obviously lend themselves to the study of practical problems of change, of the human factor in technological development, much better than did earlier interests. As the need for an applied anthropology has become increasingly apparent, and as administrative structures for the utilization of anthropologists have come into being, so has the discipline's development better prepared it to accept an active role in directed culture change programs.

APPLIED ANTHROPOLOGY IN ADMINISTRATIVE SETTINGS

During the half-century since applied anthropology began to be a recognizable subdiscipline, the kinds of things anthropologists have done in helping to direct change have evolved significantly. What applied anthropology has been at a given time and place has depended on the state of development of the science, on the availability of anthropologists willing to accept applied assignments, and on the existence of agencies of change that recognize the anthropological contribution and are willing to pay for it. England, until recently possessed of an immense colonial empire, was faced with the need to administer vast numbers of dependent peoples with relatively few colonial officials. As we would expect, in that country applied anthropology was conceived from its inception as the utilization of social, cultural, economic, religious, and other data about native peoples, largely gathered by anthropologists or by government officials trained in anthropology, in the development of improved colonial administration and especially of that form known as Indirect Rule, in which maximum use was made of indigenous personnel and traditional governmental mechanisms. Various colonial administrations supported government anthropologists or subsidized anthropological research, and new colonial administrators received anthropological training as a part of their preparation, all with the end of understanding better the dynamics of native life, and of translating this understanding into action.

Nigeria, for example, had a Government Anthropologist prior to World War I, and from about 1920 until the dissolution of the Empire, British colonies in varying degrees utilized social anthropologists to aid with native administration and, to a much lesser extent, with developmental problems. This type of applied anthropology came into being because the anthropological knowledge of the period was pertinent to the rule of dependent tribal peoples, because trained anthropologists from British and Commonwealth universities were available to work on such problems, and because colonial and home office governments were willing to give financial, practical, and moral support to anthropological investigations. The two cases that follow illustrate the early anthropological approach to colonial administration problems.

The Golden Stool. In April, 1900, warriors of the powerful Ashanti nation of the Gold Coast, a British West African colony (now independent Ghana), besieged a British garrison at the inland city of Kumasi. The siege was not lifted until mid-July, and fighting continued until the end of the year, when the Kingdom of Ashanti was annexed to the British Empire. Her Majesty's forces suffered over 1,000 casualties; those of the Ashanti are unknown, but certainly far greater. The immediate cause of this "little" war was the British demand that the Ashanti surrender a Golden Stool they were rumored to possess.

The story behind this event began early in the eighteenth century. At Kumasi, the capital city of Ashanti, a famous priest-magician drew from the sky a wooden stool of conventional design, partially covered with gold. This, he told the king and assembled multitude, was sent by the Sky God as the repository of the soul of the nation; it would make them a great and powerful people, but should it ever be captured or destroyed, Ashanti would perish. Thereafter the Golden Stool was the most cherished Ashanti possession. It was carefully guarded, and once a year carried with pomp and splendor in a public parade, as visible evidence of divine favor. The stool was placed on a hide and never allowed to come into direct contact with the ground. Nor did the king sit upon it, as upon a throne. Rather, on rare occasions, he made pretense of sitting on it, but then sat on his own stool, resting only his arm on the sacred Golden Stool. With the passage of time the Ashanti nation expanded and conquered many neighboring tribes. Each victory confirmed the prophecy of the priest-magician, and increased the reverence manifest toward the stool.

In 1873 the British signed a peace treaty with the Ashanti after capturing and burning Kumasi. But in 1893 King Prempeh refused to accept a British protectorate. British arms prevailed: Kumasi again was occupied, and King Prempeh was exiled. Meanwhile the Golden Stool was hidden in a forest village. The new colonial administrators mistakenly assumed that the stool was the symbol of royal power, the equivalent of a European crown or sceptre, and felt it necessary to obtain it to solidify their control of Ashanti. When an Ashanti traitor at the last minute failed in his promise to lead the British to the hiding place, the Governor of the Gold Coast demanded in open assembly that the stool be brought to him so that he, the representative of the queen, might *sit* upon it. This insult to the repository of the soul of the nation led to the hostilities described.

The stool remained safely hidden until 1921 when, because of the unfounded belief that the British again were searching for it, it was hurriedly buried in an unmarked spot. A short time later it was uncovered in the course of road building, but only a few Ashanti were witnesses. A degree of Ashanti cultural disintegration is indicated by the fact that these men began stripping the stool and selling the gold ornaments. The desecration came to light only when an old woman who previously had seen the stool recognized an ornament offered for sale and reported it to the proper authorities. The culprits, when the Ashanti chiefs and people learned what had happened, would have been killed had not the British intervened. But this time official policy was quite distinct: colonial administrators limited their intervention to seeing that the accused received a fair trial by a native court, and to insisting on banishment rather than capital punishment. No attempt was made to obtain the stool, which in the past had been so eagerly desired.

What caused this dramatic shift in policy? Captain R. S. Rattray, first Government Anthropologist in the Gold Coast, had begun his investigations a few months earlier. He had discovered the true nature of the Golden Stool and its meaning to the Ashanti people. The confidential memorandum he submitted to the government at the time of the discovery of the desecration of the stool was accepted as the basis of government policy, with the happy outcome described (Rattray 1923: 287–293).

The Vailala Madness. In the early stages of contact with Western culture many of the native peoples of New Guinea have experienced recurring mass hysteria movements known by the generic phrase "Cargo Cult." These movements are particularly likely to occur when tribal peoples have recognized the merit of much of the material culture of Europeans, perhaps learned in mission stations, but when at the same time they perceive the magnitude of the threat to their traditional way of life, and they fear for the future. In the common form of Cargo Cult native sacred objects are destroyed, ritual is abandoned, and secular elements are substituted. Above all it is believed that the ancestors will return on a great ship laden with desirable "cargo," and that they will drive out the Europeans.

In 1922 F. E. Williams was appointed Government Anthropologist in Papua, an Australian Mandated Territory. His first major study was of the Vailala Madness, a Cargo Cult religious movement which for ten years had disturbed the administration of Papua. Williams concluded that the movement continued because Christianity had not proven to be a sufficient substitute for the native forms it replaced, that it constituted no serious threat to the political stability of the territory, and that the government should not intervene, but allow it to run its course. The Lieutenant Governor of Papua, in spite of personal beliefs to the contrary, accepted Williams' analysis and recommendations, and no action was taken.

Williams' appraisal proved correct. When he revisited the area ten years later he found that the movement had largely, although not entirely, disintegrated. The destruction of native property had ceased, native rituals were being reintroduced, mass hysteria had disappeared, and the natives were peaceful. By contrast, in other places where government had intervened to suppress Cargo Cult movements, violence and bloodshed had resulted (Williams 1923, 1934; Rosenstiel 1954).

Anthropologists also have been and are being used in projects involving dependent peoples in non-colonial situations. In Mexico, Guatemala, and the Andean countries, large minority Indian populations present special problems with respect to health, education, and general welfare. Isolated by language and culture from the mainstreams of national development, they have not shared in full measure the benefits accruing to their fellow citizens as a consequence of industrialization and developing national infrastructures. Most of these countries have National Indian Institutes charged with aiding Indian minority groups in their development. One of the most interesting examples of the work of such an institute is outlined in the following account of the Papaloapan resettlement project in Mexico.

The Papaloapan Resettlement Project. Beginning shortly after World War II the Mexican government began a monumental program of dam building for flood control and irrigation. Millions of acres of new land have been brought under cultivation, and Mexico has changed from a food importing to a food exporting nation, in spite of doubling its population, in a little over twenty years. But, as in all cases of technological development, whether dam building, urban renewal, or freeway construction, hardship has resulted for some people, and a humane government is one that plans early to minimize human suffering.

The Papaloapan Valley Project, which began in 1947, was the first major activity in this continuing program in Mexico. The project was modeled on the Tennessee Valley Authority in the United States and had as its goal raising the standards of living of thousands of Mexicans by permitting more efficient exploitation of the natural resources of the valley. But the human price was the inundation of large numbers of Mazatec, Chinantec, and Popoloca

Indian villages, which had existed since pre-Conquest times on the eastern escarpment of the Sierra Madre Oriental, in the States of Oaxaca and Veracruz. Resettlement on new lands was essential. The Mexican government wisely placed this task in the hands of the National Indian Institute, which combines both administration and technical assistance in its function of assisting Mexican Indian minorities to incorporate themselves more effectively into the national life of the country, at the same time helping them to preserve those aspects of traditional life which the Indians wish to keep and which are consistent with the other goals of the program. The Institute maintains community development centers in many parts of the country, where research is carried out on the problems involved, and where knowledge acquired is applied to improving agriculture, housing, communication, health, and education. The Mexican anthropologist, Alfonso Villa Rojas, who was placed in charge of the relocation program, has described the steps whereby several thousand Mazatec Indians were successfully moved from old to new homes. This mass migration, he points out, was not merely a simple geographical movement, but rather a transition from a tribal way of life to civilization. Such major changes in culture are usually far more disruptive than simple migration.

To minimize the traumatic effects on the Mazatecs of losing their home lands, Professor Villa Rojas and his anthropological assistants first studied the traditional Mazatec way of life. They recognized that when the history, social structure, religious beliefs, political organization, and many other aspects of life were known, it would be possible to foresee many of the points of strain that inevitably would accompany the abandonment of old homes and ways of living. Only then would it be feasible to make detailed plans for resettlement.

When the time came to plan concretely for the change, the anthropologists sought out the true leaders of each community (rather than the nominal leaders, often political appointees with little influence) and made them their allies in explaining to others the need for the move and the advantages to be gained. These leaders were taken to inspect the lands proposed for new villages, and as far as possible their wishes concerning the areas to be colonized were respected. From the study of social organization it had become apparent that every effort would have to be made to maintain the essential unity of previous village groupings: inhabitants of one *municipio* (a political, and in this case cultural, division) were not to be mixed with inhabitants from another. Furthermore, it was recognized that the Indians had meaningful ties not only with neighbors in their own villages, but also with friends and relatives in adjacent villages. It was therefore found desirable to maintain traditional spatial relationships insofar as possible among groups of villages in the new setting. During all preparations the goal of the anthropologists was not only to plan wisely *for* the Indians, but to plan *with* them and to obtain their views and cooperation.

To this end, houses built for the Indians in the new villages made use of local materials, but they represented an improvement in hygiene, sanitation, and convenience over the old ones. Schools and churches were erected in the new communities, and educational and health services were expanded beyond what had existed in the old villages. After resettlement, provision was made for people to return from time to time to their old homes (before they were inundated), thus easing the psychological shock of an abrupt move. As people became more familiar with their new surroundings and recognized the advantages in the new villages, requests to return "home" diminished.

The enterprise was not carried out without mistakes or without bitterness on the part of some of the Indians. But it is clear that as a result of careful planning based on good social and cultural information, the movement was accomplished with far less disruption than has accompanied similar undertakings in other places (Villa Rojas 1955).

APPLIED ANTHROPOLOGY IN TECHNOLOGICAL DEVELOPMENT

Conditions promoting the growth of applied anthropology in the United States have differed significantly from those in England and in the Spanish American countries with large Indian populations. Because the United States lacked a colonial empire, and refused to recognize until fairly recently that American Indians required special treatment based on an understanding of their cultures, the administrative problems of dependent peoples have constituted a relatively small part of the American applied anthropological experience. American anthropologists, of course, worked on this type of problem in the Bureau of Indian Affairs as far back as 1934, in the Japanese relocation centers administered by the War Relocation Authority during World War II, and in the Trust Territory of Micronesia, taken from Japan in World War II.

But most American applied anthropology has dealt with the kinds of problems sketched in the first pages of this chapter: problems of the relationships between technological development and the social, cultural, and psychological characteristics of the people who are changing, and problems of the personnel of organizations charged with bringing about change. The major stimulus to the development of this type of applied work has been the postwar awareness of the underdeveloped world, now composed of independent countries with tremendous economic, political, and social problems to be solved if stable governments are to be established. In order to help achieve this goal, of stable governments capable of promoting rapid and orderly economic and social growth, the United States has already spent about one hundred billion dollars in technical aid. Other governments, private foundations, and international agencies such as the United Nations, have spent smaller but significant amounts on the same kinds of projects.

This has given rise to what may be called contemporary applied anthropology since, regardless of the nationality of the anthropologist or the country in which he works, the pattern of his utilization is the same. He does research in directed culture change problems because the importance of the sociocultural dimension in technological change and modernization is increasingly recognized, and because the agencies that carry out these programs are willing to spend money for sociocultural information. Since 1950, large numbers of American anthropologists and lesser numbers from other countries have worked in international, crosscultural technical aid programs in such fields as health, education, community development, and agriculture, and writings on these efforts form the largest block of applied anthropological research to be found anywhere in the world.

But it is erroneous to assume that all, or even most, applied anthropological work now occurs in an international setting. The kinds of problems so dramatically visible when, for example, new health measures are made available to peoples previously dependent on folk remedies and indigenous curers, also exist, perhaps in less extreme form, within any complex society. In the United States, with large numbers of minority group members, and with several social classes each characterized by distinctive patterns, subcultural differences present problems in the improvement of health, educational, and welfare services quite comparable to those found in newly developing countries. So today in the United States increasing numbers of anthropologists are found in professional schools of public health, medicine, nursing, education, and social welfare, where their teaching and research activities are directed to the sociocultural problems of each of these fields.

The examples given on pages 15–21 illustrate how applied anthropology initially dealt largely with problems of the administration of dependent peoples. In contrast, the summaries that follow illustrate contemporary applied anthropology, in which sociocultural and psychological factors in directed culture change programs are the foci of attention.

Latin American Public Health Programs. The first major international technical aid program of the United States government began in 1942 when the Institute of Inter-American Affairs initiated cooperative developmental ventures with Latin American governments in the fields of public health, agriculture, and education. In public health, a particularly successful enterprise, work was carried out (and in some places is still being carried out) in environmental sanitation, health education, the control of specific diseases such as malaria and yaws, and general preventive medicine. The American type of city or county health center, previously lacking in most of Latin America, was an especially important part of the early programs. The typical center was designed according to American concepts to offer maternal and child health services, control of communicable diseases, laboratory analyses, dental care, home visits by public health nurses, environmental sanitation control exercised by sanitarians, and vital statistics analysis. Large numbers of American personnel, representing almost all fields in medicine and public health, were detailed to Latin American posts. Many Latin American health specialists were given the opportunity to visit the United States, to observe American methods, to take courses in their special fields, or to receive longer-term training. As a result of American participation in these programs, Latin American health ministries were aided significantly in the development of their nascent health services.

In 1943 the Smithsonian Institution, as part of the same Good Neighbor Policy that produced the Institute of Inter-American Affairs, established a small division known as the Institute of Social Anthropology, whose personnel taught in Latin American institutions of higher learning. They also worked with local anthropologists and students in making analyses of Latin American communities, which were published in monograph form. These anthropologists, by reason of having lived, taught, and done research in Latin America, came to know a great deal about the basic cultural patterns of the countries in which they were stationed, and their knowledge included popular medical beliefs and practices, one of the traditional topics of anthropological investigation. At the end of the first ten years of the Institute of Inter-American Affairs' cooperative health work, the United States Public Health Service carried out a major six-month-long evaluation of all aspects of the work. Five of the Smithsonian Institution's anthropologists were invited to be members of the evaluation team, to analyze the cultural and social problems encountered in introducing new medical services and concepts into traditional communities.

Most of the anthropological analysis was directed at health centers, the keystone of the program. Although most health centers attracted large numbers of clients, sometimes they were not utilized to capacity, nor by people whose health needs could be met by them. Medical personnel asked the anthropologists: What can you tell us about cultural and social factors that will help explain the attitude of people toward health centers, why they accept or do not accept services, why they follow or do not follow instructions given them? What can you tell us about the general relationships between cultural patterns and health services?

The anthropologists decided that there were two major problem areas. The first involved the whole complex of beliefs, attitudes, and practices associated with health, prevention of disease, disease causation and curing — in the broadest sense, "folk medicine." The second involved the nature of a health bureaucracy, its premises, its planning, and the quality of relationships existing among health personnel in various jobs, and between them and the clients they serve.

The anthropologists found that even in cities folk medical beliefs and practices are a vigorous institution, often in conflict with the teachings of scientific medicine. Particularly significant is a dichotomy — subsequently confirmed in studies in other parts of the world — in the minds of people: they believe there are some kinds of illness that scientifically trained physicians can treat more effectively than folk medical curers; these usually are those that lend themselves to spectacular cures with antibiotics and other modern forms of treatment. But they also believe there are many kinds of illness, such as evil eye, fright, and others essentially emotional in origin or folk etiology that doctors not only cannot treat, *but whose very existence they deny*. Mothers who believe a child is afflicted by the evil eye are understandably reluctant to take the child to a person who insists there is no such illness. The anthropologists concluded that doctors should never ridicule or deny folk medical beliefs, and that they might if possible use the phraseology of popular medicine in order to make their explanations clearer to patients.

With respect to bureaucracy and planning, the anthropologists discovered a principle that has become axiomatic in the best tech-

nical aid programs: you cannot transplant an institution un-
changed from one culture to another and expect it to function as
effectively as in the place where it developed. In the case of public
health centers, the organizational and philosophical relationship
between preventive and curative medicine was the issue. In the
United States good curative medical services developed under
private auspices relatively early in the country's history. Public
health in its contemporary form came later, and since it is largely
a government enterprise, it has had to avoid offending the vested
interests of private medical practice. It has therefore concentrated
on preventive medicine, in the form of environmental sanitation,
immunization, maternal and child health services, and the like.
The pattern of curative medicine as largely private and preventive
medicine as largely public therefore grew up in response to the
conditions of American society. American health advisers in Latin
America naturally followed this pattern in their thinking and recommendations, with the result that new public health centers built
as cooperative enterprises followed the American pattern, emphasizing preventive to the relative neglect of curative medicine.

But medical needs are quite different in most Latin American
countries. There are far fewer practicing physicians per capita,
and because of widespread poverty the average Latin American
of the lower socioeconomic classes simply never developed the
pattern of regularly consulting a physician. When health centers
were first established in Latin American cities, potential clients
quite logically assumed they would receive curative medical attentions, which they recognized as their greatest need. When they
discovered the emphasis on preventive rather than curative services, many lost interest because they felt the centers did not meet
their wants. A health service pattern that is a logical response to
American needs often makes very little sense in the Latin American setting. The anthropologists therefore recommended that the
sharp American dichotomy between curative and preventive services not be followed in Latin America. They felt that, if the
immediate curative needs of clients could at least partially be met
in health centers, this would instill confidence and result in more

interest in preventive programs such as pre- and postnatal treatment and infant immunization. In other words, they were convinced that health services in Latin American countries should be designed to meet local needs rather than rigidly following institutional patterns developed to solve North American problems.

A number of other recommendations based on anthropological analyses were included in the report of the evaluation teams. These aroused wide interest in social and cultural aspects of public health practice among health personnel, and resulted in a number of modifications in planning and programming (Foster 1953a, 1953b; Simmons 1955; and Oberg and Rios 1955 describe specific analyses that formed a part of this research).

Fishermen in Surinam. In 1956 the Surinam government built thirty-five new homes for river bank fishermen in the village of Coppename Point. Each was raised on piles, local style, and had two bedrooms, a living room, a bath, and a kitchen, as well as running water, electricity, and screening. A reasonable twenty-year installment purchase plan was provided and the houses were all quickly taken up by fishermen. But by 1959 only nine fishermen continued to occupy their houses. Most of those who had signed contracts had left, and all had defaulted on payments. What had caused this rejection of superior housing and easy payments?

The American anthropologist, Kalervo Oberg, who had also worked on the public health analyses just described, was asked to find the reasons. His research revealed a number of social and economic factors that led to abandonment of the houses. The basic problem was that the designers had thought only in terms of improved housing, whereas the fishermen saw living quarters as only one among many elements in a complex economic and social operation. The fishermen needed at least fifty yards of river frontage for house and barbecue shed; for drying, repairing, and tarring nets; for boat storage; for quarters for hired hands; and for a kitchen garden and chicken house. Fish were smoked and dried in the barbecue shed, and the necessary wood was brought in by boat. When the shed was adjacent to the river bank much labor in moving wood was saved. Fishermen wanted to live near their boats, nets, and sheds, to prevent theft and depredation by dogs.

Most fishermen employed three or four hired hands, young men, "drifters," with no serious village attachments. Because fishermen work by tides and weather rather than by the clock, they often would decide to go out at two or three o'clock in the morning. A fisherman could be reasonably sure of finding the hired hands only if they slept on his property; if they slept off the property it was difficult to round them up, since one was never sure in which houses they might be passing the night.

The "improved" fishing village consisted of closely packed houses that made no provision for sleeping quarters for the hired hands or for guarding a fisherman's property. All were expected to use a cooperative barbecue shed, which was inconsistent with their individualistic habits. In short, a fisherman's operational base was found to involve much more than a living house; it was a unit of buildings and gear which had to be conveniently located, easy of access, and all visible from the living house. Failure of the planners to consult with the fishermen and to learn how their social and economic needs conformed to a tight pattern resulted in the failure of the project (Oberg and van Dijk 1960).

The Cornell Peru Vicos Project. The Hacienda Vicos is located in an intermontane Andean valley about 250 miles north of Lima, its 40,000 acres of agricultural, pastoral, and waste lands lying at elevations from 9,000 to 20,000 feet. For some years prior to 1952, the hacienda was owned by the Public Benefit Society of Huaraz, capital city of the political department of which Vicos is a part, and leased for five years or more to the highest bidder. In legal status, mode of exploitation, and socioeconomic forms, the hacienda and its population closely resembled several hundred similar Peruvian entities. It was managed by a mestizo administrator representing the Society who had nearly absolute powers over its 1,700 monolingual Quechua-speaking Indians who, together with their ancestors, had been bound to the land in slave-like serfdom since colonial times. A labor force for the agricultural and grazing operations of the hacienda was obtained by a work levy of three man days per week for each family. Families were also required to supply additional services as cooks, grooms, watchmen, shepherds, and servants. In return they were permitted to occupy a small plot of inferior land for subsistence farming. Peones who refused to obey orders could be thrown off the hacienda, leaving them destitute and without hope of employment since "troublemakers" would not be hired by other hacienda managers. The medieval quality of life is revealed by the fact that the value of the hacienda was measured by the number of peones bound to it rather than by its cultivable lands.

Except in traditional religious life the Indians had no voice in their affairs. Therefore, positions of responsibility in public affairs were lacking, leadership was poorly developed, almost no public services were maintained, cooperation between families was rare, the community was in general highly disorganized, and the standard of living on the hacienda was the lowest in the region. Many Vicosiños suffered from malnutrition, 80 per cent were infected with harmful parasites, epidemics of measles and whooping cough periodically carried off large numbers of children, housing consisted of one- or two-room windowless dirt-floored hovels, and clothing was insufficient for an inclement environment. A school of sorts had functioned since 1940, but over the eleven-year period only thirty-nine children had been enrolled and none had become literate. It would be hard to imagine a less promising community in which to attempt a modernization and development program.

Yet anthropologists at Cornell University and the Peruvian National Indian Institute believed it was worth trying. Late in 1951 the two institutions formed the Cornell Peru Vicos Project and, with a grant from the Carnegie Institution, leased the hacienda for five years and began an experiment in applied social science that has achieved world renown. The project directors made value judgments which they did not attempt to defend on scientific grounds. They assumed that cultural relativism is not absolute, and that some conditions, forms, practices, and beliefs are more functional than others in the modern world. To promote these conditions, forms, practices, and beliefs therefore is justifiable action *if* the people involved are fully informed of what is happening, *if* they have the knowledge and right to evaluate alternatives, *if* they participate fully in decisions taken, and *if* within a reasonable time they assume major leadership, policy, and power roles. In the words of the late Allan Holmberg, the project's founder and first director, the plan of operations ". . . focused on the promotion of human dignity rather than indignity and the formation of institutions at Vicos which would allow for a wide rather than a narrow shaping and sharing of values for all the participants in the social process. The principal goals of this plan thus became the devolution of power to the community, the production and broad sharing of greater wealth, the introduction and diffusion of new and modern skills, the promotion of health and well being, the enlargement of the status and role structure, and the formation of a modern system of enlightenment through schools and other media" (Holmberg, *et al.* 1965:5).

Project results to date, while perhaps not all originally desired, are impressive in comparison to community development programs in other parts of the world, and the process of modernization continues. In its totality the history of the project tells much about the problems of development and modernization of a traditional community, and it illustrates a great many of the points about the use of anthropologists in action programs that will be discussed in greater detail in subsequent chapters. The first important point is that the anthropologists, like those of the Papaloapan project in Mexico, were project administrators, with authority to make and execute decisions as well as to carry out research. This is an unusual situation in the use of applied anthropologists, and it testifies to the skill of the personnel involved that they were able to combine effectively administrative and research roles. A second important point is the pragmatic, ad hoc approach that characterized the program within the broad framework of philosophy just presented. The anthropologists accepted the fact that, since culture is an integrated whole, change programs must be integrated rather than piecemeal undertakings. But apart from this broad guide line, they felt their way as they proceeded, using available resources, keeping what worked, and abandoning what failed. A highly important fact, sometimes underemphasized in project reports, is that the Peruvian anthropologist, Mario Vázquez, had made a thorough study of the hacienda from 1949 to 1951. Thus there were an exceptionally good base line and a fund of knowledge on which to make plans and take immediate action. The intimate knowledge about people and cultural forms brought to the project by Dr. Vázquez made it possible to plan and take action at a rate impossible in a setting where such information must first be gathered. The visible beneficial results which followed prompt action (in agriculture, for example) unquestionably were important in developing community support for the project.

Four topical areas received major attention: economic development, especially agriculture; education; social, political, and administrative forms; and health. Results have been uneven, with economic and sociopolitical changes being most marked. As a consequence of improved cultivation and marketing processes, agricultural production has risen several hundred per cent, so that now there is not only sufficient food for local consumption but for sale as well, which has permitted major capital improvements and arrangements for the purchase of the hacienda by its own inhabitants. New skills in this area came so quickly that within very few years Vicosiños were much in demand as agricultural technical advisers to peones on adjacent haciendas.

In social structure and leadership, democratic elections have replaced traditional ritual appointments, and younger, literate, educated Vicosiños have assumed the new leadership roles that their cooperative system of organization requires. But this transformation came about in a gradual and orderly fashion: hacienda elders and straw bosses to direct work were retained in their customary positions of authority during the period of innovations, and only with the rise in confidence, knowledge, and aspirations on the part of the people were these positions replaced by more modern administrative and governmental forms.

In 1952 education was a need not recognized among hacienda

parents, and early success in attracting children to classes was due to the attraction to hungry people of 1,200-calorie school lunches rather than to the lure of knowledge. By 1963, 76 per cent of Vicos boys of school age were enrolled although, reflecting great conservatism, only 6 per cent of the girls attended classes. Nevertheless the project directors and other participating personnel feel that in the long run the school has been the most important force for change. During recent years a few Vicosiño boys have gone on to secondary schools in nearby cities, and the number is growing. Curiously, in spite of the participation of Peruvian and American medical doctors in many phases of the program, achievements in health have lagged behind those in other fields, and there was even an increase in the death rate between 1952 and 1963. Moreover, there has been no significant reduction in the chewing of coca leaves, consumption of alcoholic beverages has gone up with greater wealth, and anxiety levels appear to have risen.

In 1957 the Cornell Peru Vicos Project lease expired. Project personnel felt sufficient progress had been made so that the hacienda Indians could run their own affairs. The project therefore recommended to the Peruvian government that the hacienda be expropriated and made self-governing, and a decree of expropriation followed. But neither project nor government officials fully appreciated the power of vested interests. Prior to this action Peruvian publicity had been basically favorable; considerable pride, in fact, was expressed in this now-famous enterprise. But when the implications of the changes in Vicos began to be fully appreciated, land-owning classes not only in the valley but also in all Peru, including high government officials who held such haciendas, organized to stop what to them was a revolutionary move. Not until five years had elapsed, in 1962, was an arrangement finally worked out permitting the hacienda to purchase itself from its previous owner.

At least two important lessons in the problems of development are illustrated by the difficulties attendant upon acquiring the hacienda. The first is the power of vested interests to thwart change: when groups and classes who benefit from the status quo feel changes will threaten these advantages, they will oppose such changes with all their resources. The second has to do with the conditions that promote capital investment and improvements of a physical plant. After the great successes of the first five years, such actions fell to a negligible level during the litigation period when the outcome was in doubt. Any improvements, the inhabitants correctly reasoned, would simply raise the final purchase price. This situation also illustrates why land reform is so essential in much of the world, and why the production of tenant farmers often is so low: the benefits of progressive agriculture may, in fact, simply worsen the position of the tenant who undertakes them.

At present Vicos is organized as a production cooperative, in which its members receive the major economic benefits. It is a self-confident community, sufficiently attractive in a social and economic sense so that a considerable number of emigrants to the coast have returned to participate in the new opportunities. Professor Holmberg believes that "The major lesson of Vicos, for Peru as a whole, is that its serf and suppressed peasant populations, once freed and given encouragement, technical assistance and learning, can pull themselves up by their own bootstraps and become productive citizens of the nation" (Holmberg, *et al.* 1965:8). The Cornell Peru Vicos Project has not been without its scientific critics in both Peru and the United States. They point out that there are insufficient funds and personnel to extend the lessons learned to other haciendas, and that it is a costly, one-shot enterprise. Whether this is true or not, the results are impressive. Applied social science revolutionized the way of life of an indigenous group, and in so doing learned a great deal about the processes of accelerating development and modernization and about the problems of using anthropologists and other social scientists in action programs. Professor Holmberg's conviction that "the interventionist or action approach to the dynamics of culture, applied with proper restraint, may in the long run provide considerable payoff in terms both of more rational policy and better science" (Holmberg 1958:12) seems borne out by results. Vicos is justly famous, and the Cornell Peru Vicos Project will rank as a milestone in the development of applied social science (Holmberg, *et al.* 1962, 1965; Ritter 1967).

The following example is somewhat different from the preceding ones, but it conforms to the same broad pattern of utilization of sociocultural and psychological expertise to determine ways to influence behavior and produce change. Like Vicos, it has become a classic case of applied anthropology.

APPLIED ANTHROPOLOGY IN WARFARE

In World War II the United States for the first time in its history found itself fighting a modern, well-armed nation with a culture vastly different from its own and from that of Western Europe. Much Japanese behavior was difficult to understand. *Banzai* charges, *kamikaze* dive bombers, fights to death, refusal to surrender in the face of overwhelming odds, and brutal treatment of prisoners did not conform to Western ideas of warfare. It became apparent to American authorities that answers were needed to at least two types of problems in which previous military experience was of limited value: how best to prosecute a war, and how best to set surrender and occupation terms with a nation whose psychology and culture were so different from our own.

The Foreign Morale Analysis Division in the Office of War Information was organized to try to find answers to these, and other similar problems. When fully organized, thirty specialists in anthropology, sociology, psychology, and Japanese language and culture worked under the direction of Alexander H. Leighton. These scientists ultimately demonstrated that knowledge of the basic assumptions underlying Japanese culture would go far toward answering questions about the conduct of war and the terms for peace. For example, many military men believed that all Japanese soldiers were hopeless fanatics who would always prefer death to capture, and that it was pointless to make major efforts to capture and interrogate prisoners. In fact, much Japanese behavior lent credence to this belief. Division personnel studied the reasons for this strange behavior. They found that the

Japanese code of honor taught that surrender against even hopeless odds was a disgrace; a soldier taken while badly wounded and unconscious was equally dishonored and became "dead" to his former existence. There was no way by which he could hope to re-enter his earlier life. They also found that Japanese soldiers were convinced American soldiers would not take them prisoner but would execute them. Faced with this dilemma, a *banzai* charge against overwhelming enemy power was the logical way to die: a glorious rather than a dishonorable death.

When surrender propaganda stressed that prisoners would be well cared for and even allowed to work rather than remain idle, considerable numbers (although fewer than in the European theater) surrendered. The behavior of many astonished their captors. Without feeling the dishonor that American prisoners would under the same circumstances, they willingly gave precise information about their units' strength and disposition. Some were helpful in writing broadcast propaganda against their countrymen. And when the cultural basis for this strange behavior was fully appreciated, some prisoners flew as observers in American planes, spotting Japanese installations. The status-less condition of Japanese prisoners, alive, and anxious to carve out new lives (since they believed they could not return to the old ones), explained their behavior.

In considering terms for surrender and occupation, the major problem was what policy to take with respect to the Japanese emperor. Many American administrators felt that the situation was comparable to that of Nazi Germany, and that only through abolition of the prewar government, including the royal household, could a democratic Japanese government be established. But the analyses of the Division indicated otherwise. Faith in the emperor and in the divine power and way of life he symbolized remained at a very high level in the face of the most serious war reverses. Other officials might be condemned, but the emperor continued to be a symbol of the unity and virtue of Japan. Division scientists believed, consequently, that an attack on the emperor would only serve to strengthen the will to resist. They also concluded that traditional Japanese attitudes toward the authority of the emperor could be utilized constructively to further peace objectives. The structure of Japanese society was, they argued, such that an authoritarian but benevolent figurehead was essential to prevent social disintegration.

The advice of the social scientists played no small part in the decisions ultimately made. The emperor was to be inviolate, remaining the head of the Japanese government. In obedience to his call, Japanese fighters in all war theaters laid down their arms; through him, American military authorities were able to administer effectively and efficiently the occupation of a country of eighty million people. Rarely has a major policy decision paid off so handsomely (Leighton 1949).

CHAPTER 2
a model for
applied anthropology

THEORETICAL AND APPLIED SCIENCE

In Chapter 1 we considered examples of human problems in technological change of the kind that have given rise to the subdiscipline of applied anthropology, and summarized cases of the work anthropologists have done in several instances. We did not, however, define "applied anthropology" and "applied anthropologist," nor did we discuss the question of how the work of applied anthropologists differs from that of other anthropologists. In this chapter we will examine the relationship between theoretical and applied anthropology, by showing how the role of applied anthropologist fits into the wider scheme of the application of theoretical science to practical problems. By so doing we will outline the necessary conceptual framework for the following chapters, which deal with research methodology, the subject matter of applied anthropological research, the problems of integration of applied anthropologists into technical aid organizations, and the prestige level of applied anthropology as viewed by anthropologists.

At the risk of great oversimplification, we can say that science has two major aspects: *discovery*, the search for and the finding of new phenomena and new relationships between already known phenomena, which are accounted for by the formulation of hypotheses, principles, and scientific laws; and *utilization*, the application of the fruits of discovery and resulting theory in the service of mankind. The first is called "pure" or "basic" or "theoretical" science, and the second, "applied" science. In the popular mind, utilization flows directly from discovery and theory, so that the two aspects of science appear to form one process in which different kinds of personnel participate.

Chart 1   THE POPULAR CONCEPT OF APPLIED SCIENCE

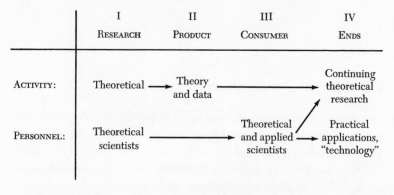

Chart 1 illustrates the relationship between pure and applied science as it is popularly conceived, dividing the research-to-use sequence into two elements, the *activity* itself and the *personnel* involved. Theoretical research is seen as carried out by theoretically oriented scientists (Column I), with a resulting "product" of theory and data (Column II). The two kinds of "consumers" of theory and data, theoretical and applied scientists (Column III), each apply the scientific product to their special "ends" (Column IV).

For the theoretically oriented scientist the corpus of scientific data and theory which characterizes his discipline at a given time is merely a progress report, a statement about the condition of the field as it is known up to that time. The product of research, therefore, is merely the jumping-off point for continuing investigation and the search for ever better and more comprehensive theory. For the applied scientist the challenge of knowledge is the search for ways to translate it into forms that will meet the needs of society: consumer goods, medical services, transportation, communication, and recreation and leisure activities. The applied scientist who converts basic knowledge into usable form is commonly thought of as the inventor or the technologist, whose peculiar genius lies in his ability to "work out" ways in which abstract theory can be translated into industrial and other goods and services which make for an ever higher standard of living.

The sequence seems simple: brilliant, theoretical minds produce basic theory, and practical, inventive minds "apply" this theory to the problems of everyday life. Hence we have "applied science." In the exact sciences, in which with some justification we can speak of scientific laws, and in which theory, although stated in problematic terms, permits prediction with certainty, this model of the application of science has a certain validity. Even here, though, it is well to remember that the model is pertinent only in the most general sense, for technology frequently has outrun theory, and in so doing has in fact been a source of that very theory from which it is supposed to draw its sustenance. For example, Pasteur's contributions to bacteriology resulted initially from trying to find solutions to the practical problems of the French silk and wine industries.

THEORETICAL AND APPLIED ANTHROPOLOGY

A great many social scientists, anthropologists among them, have accepted this model uncritically and have assumed that it also fits their disciplines. Many years ago, Radcliffe-Brown wrote that "Applied anthropology must, of course, be based on pure anthropology. What is therefore necessary in the first place is the development of the pure science by the discovery or formulation of the fundamental principles of social integration" (1931:276). Much later Lucy Mair, speaking of the relationships between theoretical and applied science, wrote that "In the field which this discussion generally covers [applied anthropology and development policies] there is no doubt as to what is meant by applied science. It is the application of principles experimentally established to the production of specific results" (1957:9).

Applied anthropology so conceived would simply have to be the application to practical ends of the data and theory of theoretical anthropology, something which could not exist until a vigorous theoretical discipline marked by laws permitting prediction had come into being. An applied anthropologist would be a technician, the social engineer who did the applying. But, as we will see shortly, the activities that have been labeled "applied anthropology" rarely if ever conform to this simple model. There is, in fact, insufficient high-level anthropological theory on which to base a successful applied branch of the discipline, if the model thought characteristic of the exact sciences must also apply to anthropology. Rather, the many and varied contributions of anthropology to practical problems are based on broad general concepts, such as culture, cultural integration, cultural dynamics, values, social structure, and interpersonal relations, and on a methodology (discussed in Chapter 3) which, like the methodologies of other social sciences, makes its unique contributions to an understanding of human behavior and its underlying motivations.

Usually an anthropologist looks upon the groups he studies in applied assignments as communities and cultures or subcultures basically no different from those he customarily analyzes, amenable to the same research methods and conceptual frameworks he uses in theoretically oriented research. The significant difference between theoretical and applied anthropology lies largely in the distinction Hauser made some years ago for the social sciences in general: ". . . not in the point of view or methods of the investigator, not in the nature of the phenomena under investigation, but rather *in the manner in which the problem is selected, in the auspices of the research and in the immediate, as distinguished from long-run, objectives*" (Hauser 1949:209 — emphasis added).

A MODEL

Hence, if the complexities of the relationship between theoretical and applied anthropology are to be appreciated, something more elaborate than the simple model is needed. This is outlined in Chart 2, in which the research-to-use sequence is broken down into the same two elements of activity and personnel portrayed in Chart 1. However, in place of a single sequence, this model shows two, one for "pure" and the other for "applied" science.

Both pure and applied research result in a "product" destined to an "end." The product of the former, ideally at least, is theory — hypotheses and generalizations — about society, culture, and human behavior. That is, the research and the conceptual framework within which it is carried out should produce ideas, insights, and hunches, which, with the data simultaneously acquired, permit theoretical interpretations of social and cultural phenomena, whose "end" is not immediate pertinence to practical programs aimed at making the world a better place in which to live. The product of the latter should be ideas, insights, comprehension, and data which lend themselves to the planning and execution of programs aimed at ameliorating specific social and economic ills, or in bringing about improved practices (as in farming or in health habits) which will benefit individuals and their society. The achievement of rather specific kinds of changes in human behavior is thus the basic "end" of applied anthropology.

Although both sequences are shown as independent, they are actually intimately related (as shown by the diagonal broken arrows), for much research carried out in applied settings has been directly relevant to basic anthropological theory and, conversely, pure research has contributed a great deal to applied problems. In fact, as we will show in Chapter 7, from a scientific point of view one of the strongest justifications for applied anthropological research is the contribution it makes to our basic corpus of data and concepts.

This model may now be examined more closely.

Chart 2 THEORETICAL VS. APPLIED RESEARCH: ANTHROPOLOGY

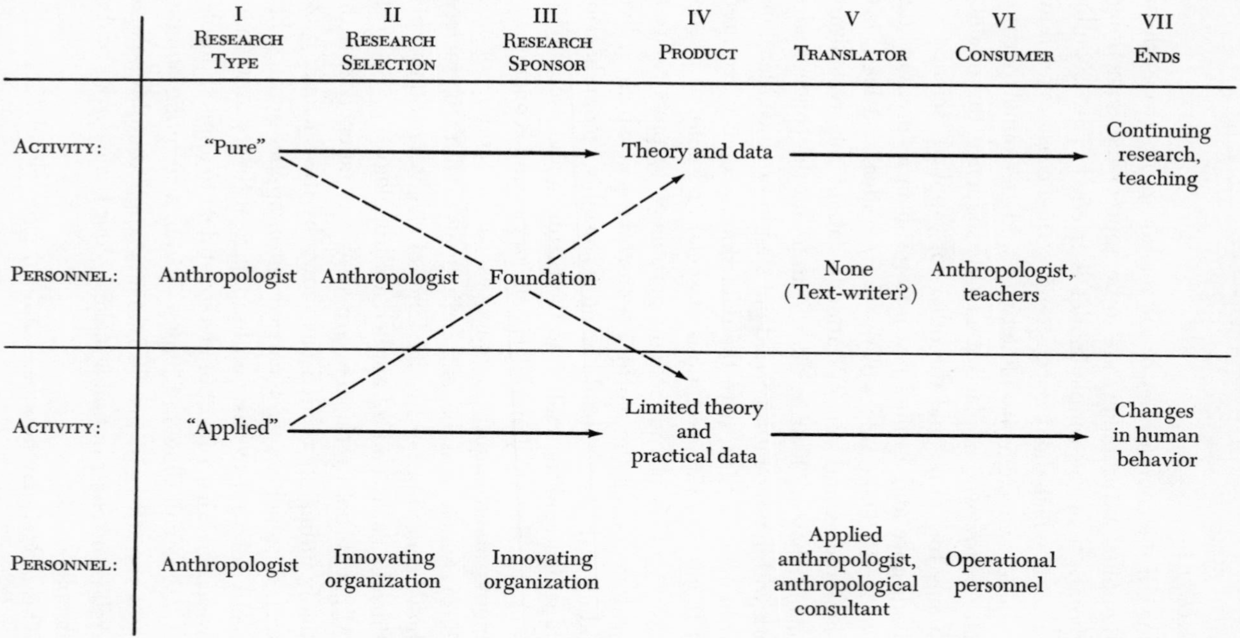

	I RESEARCH TYPE	II RESEARCH SELECTION	III RESEARCH SPONSOR	IV PRODUCT	V TRANSLATOR	VI CONSUMER	VII ENDS
ACTIVITY:	"Pure"			Theory and data	None (Text-writer?)	Anthropologist, teachers	Continuing research, teaching
PERSONNEL:	Anthropologist	Anthropologist	Foundation		Applied anthropologist, anthropological consultant		
ACTIVITY:	"Applied"			Limited theory and practical data			Changes in human behavior
PERSONNEL:	Anthropologist	Innovating organization	Innovating organization			Operational personnel	

Research Type. In both pure and applied research (Column I) the scientist is the anthropologist. Since, as pointed out in Chapter 1, "applied anthropologist" is a role rather than an occupation, the anthropologist will usually be a university teacher who combines teaching with both types of research. The important point is that, whether at the moment engaged in pure or applied research, he will have had only one kind of training and preparation. Consequently he will use the same concepts, methodology, and research methods in an applied assignment as in a theoretical analysis, and he will apply the same scientific canons of accuracy, objectivity, and freedom from value judgments. This statement also holds true for the relatively few career applied anthropologists, for they have had the same training as their academic colleagues. Clearly, the difference between pure and applied anthropology lies neither in research nor in the researchers.

Research Selection and Sponsorship. The difference first appears when we consider who decides upon a research problem (Column II) and who sponsors it (Column III). In pure research the anthropologist usually decides the problem. Selection stems from his personal interest, and his recognition that the time is ripe, or that opportunities are present, to add the next increment of knowledge to a particular theme. Pure research tends to be self-generating; science itself is the dynamic, and the ends of science are determinative.

In applied research the innovating organization charged with solving practical problems usually selects the problem, and the ends of this organization rather than those of science are determinative. The anthropologist, by accepting employment in an enterprise whose primary goals are not scientific, commits himself at least partly to the values and ends of this enterprise.

The sponsors of pure and applied research usually are different. An anthropologist pursuing his own research plans looks for support to an organization whose role in society is defined as furthering knowledge for its own sake, whose continued existence does not depend on an immediate practical "payoff." Sometimes this means research funds from a university itself. More often it is support from a private foundation such as Ford, Wenner-Gren, Carnegie, or the Social Science Research Council. Today the United States government, through the National Science Foundation and the National Institutes of Health, has become the largest supporter of pure anthropological research.

Besides giving money, institutions supporting pure research share other characteristics, the most important of which are that they do not utilize nor make a moral or legal claim on the research results stemming from their support, nor do they normally in any way limit the use of these results by the investigator. The anthropologist usually maintains full control over the data that come from his research, he decides how these data are to be presented to other interested persons, and limitations on their use, if any, are self-imposed, based on his ethical judgments.

By contrast, applied research normally is supported by the innovating bureaucracy, the client organization that sets the problem. It expects to use at least some of the research results in the furtherance of its own ends, to have a moral and legal claim on all results, and to be able to limit their use by the anthropologist who gathered them.

In practice, many sponsors of applied anthropological research operate with an extremely light hand, reserving to the scientist considerable latitude in identifying the critical factors that need investigating, within the broad framework of the practical problem, and allowing him much freedom in presenting his research data to professional colleagues in the form of articles, monographs, and papers read at professional meetings. Their concern is that the anthropologist provide them with sufficient information bearing on their problems to justify his support. Once this goal is achieved, and if there are no security problems, the anthropologist usually is free to utilize his data in whatever scientific way he chooses. A sponsoring organization may, in fact, derive considerable prestige and goodwill by a policy of allowing researchers under contract to act as professionals in presenting data and hypotheses to anthropological colleagues.

The Product of Research. The product of research (Column IV), its form of presentation to others, and its mode of utilization are rather different in pure and applied anthropology. The product of pure research, as has been shown, is science, in the form of new data, new hypotheses, new statements of regularities, new laws. Its form of presentation is determined by its major audience of other anthropologists, and scientists in closely related fields. Early and tentative results may be read as scientific papers at professional meetings. Often such papers are rewritten, perhaps in the light of professional criticism, and published as articles in professional journals. Larger bodies of data are subjected to more extensive analysis, to be published in monograph or book form. It is important that the researcher himself is charged with the scientific interpretation of his investigations and their communication to his colleagues.

The product of applied research is perhaps more varied. The results of good applied anthropological investigations include a large theoretical component; this, as the broken arrows in the model indicate, feeds into the product of pure research. But applied research, if it fulfills its aims, must also produce "practical" data and theories in the form of information, ideas, insights, and knowledge that are seen as contributing to the solution of the problems which are the concern of the sponsoring organization. And this "practical" information, the goal of the research as far as the client organization is concerned, usually cannot be communicated in the same fashion as the pure researcher communicates with his colleagues. Rather, much more of it is transferred (in the social sciences, at least), in staff meetings, in organizational conferences, and in informal, often social, settings. Much of the information is also presented in the form of memoranda that can be quickly prepared and inexpensively reproduced in small numbers, to reach the policy makers, administrators, and technicians who presumably can utilize it. To these people, the theoretical component of the research is at best of slight interest.

The Translator and the Consumer. So far, the personnel sequence in both pure and applied anthropological research is essentially the same: anthropologists with the same kind of training (often the same individual), utilizing the same research methodology and following common canons of control and objectivity, examine, observe, analyze, and interpret the meaning of a body of data. They then communicate this knowledge in ways designed to be most easily understood by the audiences for whom it is intended. But here the sequence changes. In pure research the principal "consumers" (Column VI) are the anthropologist himself, his professional colleagues in the social sciences, teachers who, whether or not they engage in similar research, are trained in social science, and the interested reading public. In contrast, the results of applied research are "consumed" by specialists representing other professions and disciplines who view these data simply as one factor among a great many orders of factors they must consider in carrying out their work. These operational personnel, as they are called on the chart, are policy makers and planners, program administrators, and technical specialists in such fields as public health, social welfare, agriculture, community development, and the like.

There is less need in pure than in applied investigation for the role of "translator" (Column V), someone who explains to the consumer the meaning of research results. When the consumer is himself a research scientist he shares a common scientific background with the original investigator, and so needs no help in interpreting new data and theory. The consumer who is not primarily a research specialist — perhaps a college teacher or a layman who wishes to know more about the subject — may find a translator helpful. A translator may be a textbook author, often the research scientist himself, or the science popularizer, a professional writer with the skill necessary to translate the ideas and data found in the monographs and papers with which the scientist communicates with his fellows into forms that require less specialized scientific preparation. So the role of translator exists in pure science, but it is less crucial to achieving major ends than in applied research.

The planners, administrators, and technical specialists who are the consumers of applied anthropological research require that data be presented to them in a form they can relate to the other factors they manipulate in their work. The often esoteric terminology of social scientists must be simplified, and the facts critical to a project must be extracted from the mass of data in which they are imbedded, and presented in a clear, succinct manner that makes obvious their implications for program planning and operations. The role of translator is essential. Not infrequently — almost always in anthropology — this role is filled by the research scientist himself. Particularly if he has been in close touch with operational personnel, and thus knows their problems well, he is the best suited of all possible people to serve as translator. In an informal way he probably has been translating throughout the research project as he meets with and talks to project administrators and technicians.

Consultants also fill the role of translators. In anthropology they are usually university professors who are called in by an action-oriented agency for a day or two, or sometimes longer, to try to relate specific anthropological data or basic theory to some problem on which the action agency is working. Sometimes consultants also do short-term research dealing with these problems.

It is at this point in the model that we can properly speak of "application" and of an "applied anthropologist." It is here that the results of a specific action-oriented research project are related to pertinent general anthropological theory and data, purged of their irrelevancies for the ends of the organization that is sponsoring the research, and presented to operational personnel in ways and in forms that permit maximum utilization. It is a mark of the youth of anthropology that the university-based scientist whose primary interest is theoretical research, but who may also engage in action-oriented research from time to time, is usually this translator who fills the temporary role of applied anthropologist. In other sciences this function has long since been assigned to recognized specialists. In the natural sciences the specialist is the industrial scientist or the industrial engineer, while in genetics he is the animal or plant geneticist. Anthropology is moving toward similar specialization, and the time will come when some anthropologists will find their major interests clustering around this type of activity. Already we are beginning to see this in medical anthropology and educational anthropology. But for some time, at least, the role of translator, of applied anthropologist, will continue to be played by the general, all-purpose anthropologist.

The responsibility of translator, whether assigned to a full-time specialist or temporarily to a university-based scientist, is by no means passive, a mechanical task of finding simple answers to social problems in technological change, and then explaining what it is all about in words and concepts the layman can understand. It is, or should be, a research role in which a high degree of creativity is exercised, and from which significant contributions to basic theory emerge. Often the anthropologist has access to groups of people he could not study in traditional research, and almost always he can learn about the workings of bureaucracy, through real "participant observation," in a way denied to most anthropologists concerned with more traditional tasks.

When a mutually satisfying personal relationship exists between the anthropologist and the administrator, the former will play a major part in the selection of research projects as well as in determination of research design, although of course ultimate authority lies with the administrator. The wise administrator knows his problems and the kinds of answers he needs to solve them, but he recognizes that the anthropologist knows better than he how to get these answers. The applied anthropologist has the responsibility of familiarizing himself with the administrator's (and the technical specialist's) needs, and then telling him what questions are to be asked (i.e., determining research design) in order to meet these needs. For these, and other reasons to be discussed later, the best applied anthropology occurs when there is a close operating relationship, with mutual respect and trust, between the anthropologist and the personnel of the organization charged with reaching specific goals.

Although it is in the role shown as translator on the model that the activities of the applied anthropologist most commonly cluster, applied anthropologists also sometimes serve as administrators. They are then themselves "consumers" of applied research, their own or that of other anthropologists. This was true of the Papaloapan resettlement scheme described in Chapter 1, where anthropologist-administrators planned and directed the work, and of the Vicos project. Anthropologists also served, as we have mentioned, as administrators in the War Relocation Authority camps in World War II, and in the Trust Territory of Micronesia following the war. There is no reason why an anthropologist — or any other scientist — should not make a good administrator. Although to the layman the scientist, apparently isolated by his ivy-covered walls from the real world of action, may appear to be the antithesis of the practical administrator, the fact is that the same thought processes, the same analytical methods, and the same judgments characterize both. Scientists and administrators alike must define their goals, decide what the significant data are, acquire these data, order them, and draw conclusions from them. Only at this point does a basic distinction appear. The scientist's task is done when he draws conclusions, i.e., advances his hypotheses. But the administrator is then faced with the most critical test of all: he must take action, based on what has gone before, and hope that his conclusions further his organization's course toward meeting its goals.

Nevertheless, although anthropologists have served as able administrators, there is general agreement among American and British anthropologists that this is not a desirable role *if* the anthropologist also expects to do research. The anthropologist's primary value in goal-oriented projects is that he can be impartial, a friend of the personnel of the bureaucracy and of the members of the target group. In exercising his obligations he does not have to reveal confidences or take action which may impinge on the freedom of others. The administrator, on the other hand, must exercise authority. People are much less apt to be frank informants if they know that the anthropologist to whom they are revealing information may subsequently change hats and use this information to their detriment (as seen by them, at least). So, although anthropologists sometimes work as administrators, this is not the major focal point of applied anthropological activities.

The Ends of Research. The "ends" (Column VII) of theoretical and applied research are distinct. For the theoretician they are additional research, and probably teaching by the anthropologist himself. Thus, the initiator of the original research, and professional colleagues similarly trained, see the sequence through to its logical end. It is an integrated activity without significant discontinuities, all comfortably within the confines of a rather tight little professional group. Anthropologists maintain control at all stages of the sequence, and they are responsible for the ethical and moral as well as the scientific aspects of this sequence. It is an essentially secure situation for the researcher: he has no outside master, and he is responsible to and judged only by his colleagues.

For the applied anthropologist, the ends of the research sequence are changes in human behavior which further modernization, technological and social development, and higher standards of living. Mexican villagers may adopt new health practices as a consequence of research about traditional beliefs which permits a more efficient government health service, or traditional farmers, following upon similar applied research, may be persuaded to adopt improved cultivation methods. But in contrast to the theoretical sequence, the anthropologist who carries out and interprets the research essentially loses control of the operation at the point where administrators and technical specialists begin to use his material. The responsibility for final action lies in their hands, and not in his. For the anthropologist working in an applied setting this loss of control is sometimes disquieting and unsettling. Since the anthropologist tends to identify more with the people who form the target group than with those in the innovating organization, he is sensitive lest in some way confidences revealed to him in the course of research may, if they reach the ears of others, injure the informants. Or he fears that the results of his research may be carelessly or even dishonestly utilized.

The best way to minimize these dangers, I believe, is for the anthropologist to have a close working relationship with the members of the bureaucracy itself. In this way, through personal friendship and through intimate knowledge of the action programs as they shape up and are executed, he can maintain a degree of informal control which in most instances is sufficient to ensure that anthropology's ethical standards are maintained.

A DEFINITION

The activities and personnel roles involved in theoretical and applied anthropology have been compared and contrasted by means of a model. This model points out how an anthropologist is best thought of as doing applied work when he has some kind of formal tie with an innovating organization oriented toward social, economic, and technological goals involving rather specific kinds of changes in human behavior. When working in such a setting, the anthropologist accepts the organization's right to determine the major research topics, in return for which he receives financial and other support. He also agrees to present his research results and the ideas stemming from them to the personnel of the organization in forms acceptable to planners, administrators, and technical specialists, rather than in the forms customarily used to communicate with members of his own discipline. It is this functional association with a nonacademic organization with goals of the type described, and the role modifications that the association requires, that makes an applied anthropologist.

The anthropologist draws upon his basic professional knowledge, of course, but only rarely can it be said that he is "applying" theory and data developed on the "pure" side of the discipline to practical problems. When his applied assignment involves investigation, he works in essentially the same way as when his interest is primarily theoretical, simultaneously bearing in mind both his own questions about human behavior and those asked by the administrators and technicians in the organization with which he is associated.

Stressing association rather than application, we can say that *"applied anthropology" is the phrase commonly used by anthropologists to describe their professional activities in programs that have as primary goals changes in human behavior believed to ameliorate contemporary social, economic, and technological problems, rather than the development of social and cultural theory.*

It may be argued, with some justification, that this definition should be broadened to include research which is neither selected nor supported by a client organization, but whose product is of immediate or potential use in an action program. Thus, Steubing's analysis of the tensions that exist in a high school, briefly summarized in Chapter 7, was not supported by an action-oriented organization. Nevertheless his observations would be extremely useful for a school system examining itself with a view to improving operations. The Institute of Social Anthropology's public health research described in Chapter 1 was, in fact, preceded by a shorter research project selected by anthropologists rather than by public health personnel, and supported by Smithsonian Institution funds. The results of this research were recognized by Institute of Inter-American Affairs personnel as significant to their health programs, and this led to the inclusion of anthropologists on the evaluation team. Because of the use immediately made of this initial research it is properly classed as applied, even though the usual bureaucratic ties did not exist. Few if any definitions can be completely comprehensive and precise, fitting all conceivable cases. The one-sentence definition above, however, seems to me to be generally accurate, and at the same time expressive of the basic differences between theoretical and applied work.

CHAPTER 3   the anthropologist's
                             methodology

METHODOLOGY: ANTHROPOLOGY'S
CONTRIBUTION TO ACTION PROGRAMS

In the preceding chapter applied anthropology was defined as a functional relationship between an anthropologist and an organization engaged in directed culture change (usually of the type found in technological development and modernization programs), rather than as a mechanical application of preexisting theory to practical problems. This definition, however, leaves unanswered the basic question of what anthropology has to offer program planners, administrators, and technical specialists if not the utilization of basic theory and data in the search for ways to facilitate change and development.

As briefly mentioned in Chapter 2, most applied anthropologists feel that their most important contribution to action programs is an unusually broad and flexible field research methodology, based on a holistic view of society and culture and using general concepts such as cultural integration, cultural dynamics, sociocultural systems in contact, and the premises underlying cultural forms as a

means to structure research and interpret results. Anthropological
field research is exploratory and wide ranging, and in contrast to
the more elaborate research methods of other social sciences, it is
relatively unstructured. But in directed culture change programs,
where the technical, social, cultural, economic, psychological, and
other pertinent factors are almost infinite and usually not recognized in advance, this exploratory quality is enormously advantageous. It vastly increases the investigator's chances of hitting
upon the critical elements in any specific situation, simply because
the anthropologist is trained to examine the entire spectrum of the
culture he studies.

THE SYSTEMS APPROACH

The concept of whole "systems" underlies the anthropological
method. The anthropologist habitually thinks of data and problems
in the context of larger units, which may be social, cultural, or economic, or more likely a combination of these and many more. A
major part of his research task is to define the boundaries of the
pertinent system, so that the outer limits, within which data and
hypotheses will be considered, can be set. Traditionally the systems have been tribes and other small communities, but units such
as minority enclaves in cities, and hospitals, business offices, factories, and foreign aid missions also are "systems" which can be
studied in essentially the same way.

Interest in systems dynamics is not, of course, limited to anthropology. It is the basis of the new discipline of "operations (or systems) research" (or analysis) and its applications in the exact
sciences, and it characterizes the other humanistically oriented
social sciences such as cultural geography and particularly psychiatry. With the exception of the obvious links between cultural
geography and cultural anthropology, however, these similarities
appear to have evolved independently. The founders of operations
research in the 1940's were concerned with military strategies, and
it is doubtful that they were even remotely acquainted with anthropological methodology. And, while Freud was cognizant of cultural
differences, his psychoanalytic approach was developed from his
clinical practice; his cultural interests came later.

ORIGINS OF THE HOLISTIC VIEW

The anthropological emphasis on systems developed from within the discipline itself, an inevitable outgrowth of the early definition of the anthropologist's primary task, which required a field rather than a laboratory approach. This task was to study and record the primitive societies of the world before they vanished. The assignment was total — find out *everything* there was to be known about the people studied. The underlying problems were assumed to be historical, and the goal was to describe and reconstruct as far as possible the histories of nonliterate peoples. Anthropology's claim to status as a social science was not made until later.

Since there were so many primitive peoples and so few anthropologists, there was no room for specialization. A single person, or at most a husband and wife team, studied social organization, religion, economics, material culture, folklore, language — and probably measured a few heads as well! Everything people did, everything they said, everything they remembered was potential grist for the anthropologist's mill.

This early definition of problem, coupled with small numbers of field workers, has provided anthropologists with the basic assumptions underlying a great deal of the work they do today. The field worker could not study so many aspects of life in isolation. He was forced — by the reality of culture — to see them in contact with one another, as parts of a whole, as facets that could be explored from a great many theoretical foci. The anthropologist found he could not study religion without quickly becoming involved in economic activities, in kinship structure, in mythology. Legal structure could not be separated from the family, from friendship patterns, from concepts of property. And material culture penetrated all aspects of life, from art to agriculture. The customary chapter divisions of classic ethnographic monographs are, of course, merely the constructs of the authors, devices to permit presentation of the data, for the data themselves — human behavior and its products — are so tightly integrated that any division is arbitrary.

So, when observing behavior, the anthropologist asks himself almost automatically, "How does this behavior bear on other activities, how does it condition or limit them, and how is it in turn affected by them?" Consciously and unconsciously his questions have to do with how the entire system works. As Rapoport puts it, the anthropologist asks of the system, "What is going on here?," rather than, "What can I demonstrate about the relationship in this situation of certain variables I have conceptually abstracted and for which I have developed precise instruments of measurement?" (Rapoport 1963:1900).

Weiss contrasts this "holistic" approach with the "analytic" approach; he sees them as complementary rather than competitive, each suitable to different types of problems. In the analytic approach, which characterizes most social sciences other than anthropology, the investigator is concerned with such things as isolating the elements of a complex situation; identifying independent, dependent, and intervening variables; and analyzing small numbers of linked relationships. He sees relationships among variables as meaningful apart from the situation itself. In the holistic approach, the investigator is concerned with the nature of the system itself rather than with particular independent-dependent variables. He wants to discover the dynamic processes that characterize the system, and how its elements integrate into a functional whole. The focal interest of the holistic investigator is, as Weiss puts it, "Taking it all together, how does the whole thing work?" (Weiss 1966:199).

The methodology of anthropology, like that of any other science, is marked by underlying assumptions rarely questioned by investigators, as well as by specific characteristics which, if not unique to it, distinguish it from its sister disciplines. Some of these characteristics and assumptions will now be considered.

SPECIAL CHARACTERISTICS OF THE ANTHROPOLOGICAL METHODOLOGY

Nomenclature. Following the natural history tradition, anthropologists describe their research activities as *field work,* in contrast to sociologists, psychologists, and other social scientists who speak of *data gathering.* More than a difference in terminology is involved. In most social sciences elaborate research projects can be designed in which the primary investigator depends largely if not entirely on research assistants whom he has instructed in the methods of gathering data. Sometimes these assistants are not even social scientists, but simply paid helpers.

In anthropological field work, however, because of the exploratory nature of the activity, and because the total spectrum of behavior and happening within the system is of real or potential importance, the anthropologist must himself participate in data gathering to an extent unmatched in the other fields. Anthropologists find that, time after time, a chance event or a near subliminal happening proves to be the key to a major hypothesis or to an insight into the functioning of the system being studied. But in order to recognize the significance of such events, the anthropologist must be on the spot, and he must be sufficiently conversant with the system to appreciate the meaning of a point that to others might seem very minor. Anthropologists, of course, to extend their own time and energy, often use field assistants who, with good supervision, can do invaluable work. But in most instances it would be impossible to design a complex anthropological research project that depended on field assistants alone for the gathering of data. To take full advantage of the research leads that continually present themselves in the field, the anthropologist needs to be on the scene most of the time.

The Personal Equation. These data-gathering imperatives introduce into anthropological field research a personal element that is poorly developed or lacking entirely in other social sciences. The social anthropologist must experience "total immersion" in the system he is studying. He does this through "participant observation": he lives in or in close association with the community under analysis, comes to know well a great many of its people, makes good friends, and occasionally acquires enemies as well. Inevitably the anthropologist's emotional involvement with the people he is studying has great bearing on the kinds of data he gathers, their validity, and their interpretation.

Field work is a chancy thing, unpredictable in the extreme. Not infrequently anthropologists find they cannot work in the community for which their research was designed and for which they prepared themselves. A single powerful individual may take a dislike to them, or the entire community may be so suspicious of all outsiders that it will have nothing to do with a nosey intruder, however harmless he may appear. In that case the anthropologist has no choice but quietly to fold his tent, steal out in the night, and try to find a more receptive community.

Even under ideal conditions the anthropologist has far less control over his research setting than do most other social scientists. Random samples are rare, except for the simplest census data. An anthropologist finds he must work with informants willing to be his friends, with whom he can establish rapport. Consequently, at the beginning of a field trip, it is never possible to predict the results, whether the anthropologist will have a rich body of data or a skimpy collection of oddments which he has acquired in spite of poor rapport with the people.

Culture Shock. Obviously the anthropologist in the field, especially in the early period when he is not yet sure of acceptance, is subject to extreme emotional pressure. Some field situations can be frightening, raising fears for personal safety, and at the very least the anthropologist knows he is undergoing a severe professional test in which he must rely entirely on his own resources. He is expected to return home with extensive and excellent data of theoretical import, but during the early months of his work he cannot be entirely sure that he will achieve this goal.

The common result of this situation is "culture shock," the same psychological malfunctioning as that experienced by most people who find themselves in strange settings, in which they recognize neither the cues of the culture nor the appropriate responses to the cues, and in which they feel themselves under pressure to achieve. In greater or lesser degree all anthropologists experience culture shock, at least on their first field trips and not infrequently on subsequent trips as well (Oberg 1954; Foster 1962: 187–194).

Flexibility in the Anthropological Methodology. The relatively unstructured quality of most anthropological research, its lack of

rigidity in design, stands in striking contrast to the research of
other social sciences. This flexibility, which some people see as a
mark of scientific immaturity, is in fact one of the strengths of the
methodology. It permits the anthropologist in the midst of his research to make major changes in his plans, to modify his original
design, and even to strike out in an entirely new direction if he
catches the scent of something he feels to be important. Anthropological field work continually generates new ideas, new problems, and new hypotheses, as a consequence of the data that flow
in, and of the experiences of the investigator. University professors
are not in the least surprised or disapproving when, after a year in
the field, a graduate student returns with data and hypotheses
that bear little or no relationship to his original research plan. It
is assumed, and students are taught, that the ability to recognize
new leads in the field is one of the marks of a fine anthropologist.
This research flexibility is one of the most important elements in
developing and maintaining a vigorous anthropology, and it is
one of the most valuable characteristics of the discipline for applied research.

SOME ASSUMPTIONS UNDERLYING
THE ANTHROPOLOGICAL METHODOLOGY

Assumptions about Racial Differences. Anthropologists assume
that differences in cultural forms and levels of development are
due to historical and cultural circumstances, and that they do not
reflect racial potentials. While anthropologists recognize great
differences in individual abilities and talents, they assume that the
average innate intellectual capacity of all large, racially homoge-
neous groups is essentially equal. Explanations for the rise and fall
of empires, for the cultural backwardness of some peoples, and for
the rapid development of others, they believe, are to be found in
history and not in race.

The Case Study Method. Whether the object of analysis is a
peasant community or a mental hospital, the anthropologist assumes that, although in some ways he is dealing with a unique
phenomenon, he is also working with a representative of a generic

type. Hence, hypotheses and generalizations which he develops from this one instance can be extended, as heuristic devices, to other communities assumed to be similar, to be tested, accepted, rejected or modified. We may note, however, that this justification for doing what Raymond Firth calls "micro-sociology" is an ex post facto rationalization which reflects the current sociological orientation of much anthropology. Earlier anthropologists studied tribes and other communities simply to find out what was there, and to record the way of life.

The Comparative Approach. Since most research produces case studies, it follows that comparison of the results of one study with those of similar studies is essential in order to exploit fully the significance of research. Comparative analysis has told us much about the structures of societies in general and about role relationships. It has also contributed greatly to our knowledge of basic change processes. We have isolated a number of dynamic regularities in change which appear to be independent of specific cultures, and which are inherent in all situations in which readily identifiable factors exist. Knowledge of these regularities is essential to the planning of change, since it makes possible prediction of what is likely to happen in a given situation.

For example, it is clear that when subsistence farmers turn to cash crops or wage labor, which makes it necessary for them to buy much of their food, their dietary problems become more serious. Planners who know this fact will — or should — consider nutrition as one of the cultural areas for which they must make provision when they upset traditional subsistence agricultural patterns. Again, we know that the personality of the "change agent," that is, the technical specialist, and especially his ability to establish friendships with the people toward whom he directs his message, has much to do with his success. Target group members often innovate, not because they are convinced of the value of the change agent's ideas, but because they feel that friendship obligations require them to do so. Recognition of this motivation obviously emphasizes the importance of personal qualities as well as of the technical qualifications of change agents.

Cultural Patterns. Anthropologists assume an underlying logic, a sense-making integration, and a patterned distribution in the phenomena of the institutions they study. They assume that one of their major tasks is to uncover these primary patterns and to describe the ways in which they apply to the institutions of the groups in question. They also assume that both data and patterns conform to limited possibilities, that the range of variation is finite. Otherwise, of course, comparison would be meaningless.

The Significance of All Data. Since anthropologists believe that a culture or social system is a logical, integrated, holistic phenomenon in which the parts fit together in meaningful patterns, they assume that every bit of data in the system has meaning and ultimately may be fitted into patterns and hypotheses. Obviously this doesn't mean that all data are immediately significant to every problem; if this were so, anthropological research would be impossible simply because of the weight of detail. It does mean that the time and context may arrive during a major study when data previously thought to be insignificant will acquire great importance. This explains the anthropologist's wide-ranging, insatiable curiosity which, in a major study, produces far more data than will ever be used. Such curiosity does not reflect a lack of mental discipline, an antiquarian bent; rather, it is basic to anthropological methodology and essential to the fullest success.

Many Data Gathering Techniques. Since anthropologists wish to acquire as many and as varied data as possible, and since the spectrum of behavior that interests them is usually very broad, it is logical for them to use a great variety of techniques to gather information. Above all, they look and listen, ask questions, and, through open-ended interviews, probe more deeply. In community studies they almost certainly take a census and work out kinship and other social relationships. They may use projective tests, take down life histories on tape recorders, and utilize whatever historical and local statistical data are available. Increasingly anthropologists also use questionnaires which, however, they see as adjuncts to other methods rather than as the primary data gathering technique itself. For anthropologists have learned that the actual behavior of people does not always coincide with the answers they give when confronted with direct questions. Discrepancies sometimes stem from the informant's desire to conceal the truth; other times he simply wants to give answers he believes will please the researcher. Discrepancies also occur because an informant may not be able to think abstractly about a particular question. For example, in my research in Tzintzuntzan I am attempting to establish the precise use and meaning of words people use to describe human character. One question I ask is whether such a word also can be used to describe animal traits. Once I asked an informant if an animal can be *intelligent*. She replied negatively — that an animal can be *clever*, but never intelligent. A few minutes later, looking at several kittens playing on the floor, she remarked, "These kittens are very intelligent, aren't they?"

The Use of Language. Anthropologists take it for granted that they must speak and understand the language of the people they study if their research results are to meet the exacting canons of excellence of contemporary field work. Control of the language is essential, obviously, for primary communication, for asking questions and understanding answers. It is also important to be able to eavesdrop, to understand what people are saying among themselves. Beyond these uses, anthropologists see language as an indispensable tool that aids them in penetrating the culture and psychology of a people. When, as in Tzintzuntzan, people customarily speak of life as a "struggle" or "contest," they are telling me something about their cognitive orientation, about the way they perceive the universe about them. And when they deny they believe in witchcraft, but insist on using euphemisms to talk about the subject, they suggest that the topic is more sensitive than they wish me to believe. Although much good ethnological field research has been done through interpreters, today anthropologists consider preparation in the language of the group they will study a basic part of their training.

An Applied Anthropological Assumption. In addition to the foregoing assumptions which characterize all anthropological field research and analysis, applied anthropologists subscribe to an additional premise: in order to direct change most successfully, build on what already exists. They assume a logical explanation for all behavior in the groups they study, even though, with the passage of time, reasons that were once valid may no longer be well suited to contemporary needs. Applied anthropologists obviously are not opposed to change, a criticism sometimes directed at anthropology. But they do not necessarily approve of change plans simply because such plans fit a planner's or a technician's idea of the desirable. In analyzing a community in order to aid in introducing new behavior forms, applied anthropologists try to find the institutions and customs which have growth potential and which can serve as a base for innovation.

To illustrate, most peasants are highly individualistic in outlook and attitudes, and cooperation for the general good of their community is relatively rare. Doctrinaire community development programs are based on the assumption that progress comes through cooperation, and that a primary task is to find ways to develop a cooperative sense in peasant communities. Perhaps because of this rigidity in doctrine, community development has been less successful than one might wish. Most applied anthropologists believe that the first innovations presented to a peasant community should be ones about which individuals can decide for themselves and adopt without waiting for the entire community to come to a joint decision. That is, most suggest building on the preexisting sense of individualism, rather than waiting for the emergence of a sense of cooperation.

EXPLICIT AND IMPLICIT CULTURAL ASSUMPTIONS

One way of looking at societies and cultures (and subcultures, too, such as bureaucracies) is so important to anthropologists and to the analyses they make, and so little explored, as to require special attention. I refer to the unquestioned assumptions, the basic premises, the unrecognized postulates that underline the cultural forms and individual behavior of the members of a group. All members of a group share a common cognitive orientation, a com-

prehension and interpretation of the world around them which, in
effect, set the terms and conditions on which they feel life is lived.
Some aspects of this common cognition are fairly explicit, in that
they are found at an overt, conscious level and can be verbalized
by most members of the society. Middle and upper class Americans, for example, have no difficulty in expressing their assumption
that manual labor has dignity, that hard and intelligent work usually is rewarded with success, and that "people are basically alike
all over the world." (Needless to say, it is the presence of an
assumption, rather than whether it is in fact correct, that is
significant.)

Other aspects of cognitive orientations are more covert and subconscious; they represent assumptions and premises so deeply imbedded in the individual's mind that normally he is not aware of
them. The cognitive judgment of many peasants that all good things
in life exist in limited, unexpandable amounts, and that consequently the good fortune of one is at the expense of others (discussed at greater length in Chapter 4), illustrates the concept of
implicit premises.

Implicit and explicit premises, of course, represent polar points
of a continuum rather than a hard and fast dichotomy, and what is
explicit for one person may be implicit for another. We can, therefore, think of the totality of an individual's premises as points
along a continuum, some clustering toward the implicit and others
toward the explicit. Personally, I see the implicit, covert level of
premises as more determinative of behavior than the explicit, overt
level, in the same way that the subconscious levels of the psyche
take precedence over the conscious levels in determining individual personality. The influence of implicit premises upon behavior can be elucidated by an analogy with grammar. Most
people normally do not think about grammar — which means
patterned regularities in language — in daily speech. In fact, the
great majority of people do not even know there *is* structure in
their language. Yet everyone by the mere act of conversing be-
haves as if he were bearing these regularities uppermost in his
mind. Rules, regularities, and symbolic meanings in speech, of

which the speaker is totally unaware, or momentarily unconscious, *determine* how he speaks, i.e., his linguistic behavior. In the same way, most of us are unaware of the implicit premises of our cultures, and even when we begin to fathom them, in our daily lives we think little of them. Yet, as with speech, we *act* as if they were consciously present, continually uppermost, in our minds.

Cultural forms can therefore be thought of as a function of or a response to the shared assumptions — and particularly the implicit assumptions — of the members of a group. They condition attitudes about interpersonal relations, about roles, and about status. They determine how people relate to their economic systems, and how they view work and its rewards. Cultural premises underlie feelings about religion and the supernatural, they determine philosophies of life, they establish forms of logic, and they express basic values. If we know the premises that characterize a culture (or a subculture such as a bureaucracy), we have something firm to which to tie our analyses of behavior. In peasant conservatism, for example, we see not just an exasperating trait but an attitude that is entirely rational, given the peasant's view of the world about him. And in many hospital routines we see reflected the assumption that schedules must fit the convenience of doctors and other staff members rather than promote the comfort of patients.

It is important to remember that, as forces determining behavior, both explicit and implicit premises may be correct or incorrect. It is not their truth or error that counts, but rather *what people believe or feel to be true*. Many of the developmental problems facing the world today are due to the fact that premises that at one time had a great deal of validity are today outdated, no longer fitting reality. Yet the behavior these premises engendered at an earlier date lingers on, as a cultural lag, discouraging innovation and encouraging people to cling to rules that worked well in the past. This is true of peasant villagers, and it is equally true of bureaucracies, where standard operating procedures are rarely if ever geared to contemporary demands.

In the practice of applied anthropology, a most important task is to determine the premises underlying the behavior both of the members of the innovating organization and of the group toward which its efforts are directed. When we know the professional premises of doctors, nurses, agricultural experts, educators, and community developers (as well as the basic national cultural premises they share with their fellow citizens), we can understand better their behavior, and we can point out why, at times, they may insist on single-minded approaches to complex problems. And when we understand the cultural premises of people who are objects of directed change programs, we can better plan the modes of presentation of new ideas, and identify the innovations most likely to be accepted. In the following two chapters, the ways in which an understanding of premises bears upon change, and the ways in which this understanding can aid in program planning are explained in greater detail.

THE FOCI OF APPLIED ANTHROPOLOGICAL RESEARCH

A great deal of applied anthropological research covers a wider range of phenomena and situations than do conventional anthropological field studies. In most instances of social anthropological investigation, the anthropologist selects a tribe or community and directs his attention to uncovering the structure and function of its institutions and the dynamic processes that bring about change. If he is concerned with the problems of acculturation, the effect of a donor culture on the group he studies will be of importance to him. In the same fashion an anthropologist may also study a subcultural system, such as a hospital, a business office, a factory, or a government bureau. In either type of study the anthropologist's primary interest is focused on the single system he has defined as his research project and, with minor exceptions, he tends to ignore the points at which this system articulates with other systems.

But when an anthropologist participates in a directed culture change program, he must be concerned with a minimum of two cultures or social systems, the *directed* and the *directing*, as well as the point at which they come together and *interact*, each with an impact on the other. The structural characteristics of directed culture change programs therefore define three basic foci of investigation to which the anthropologist must give attention if he is to do his best work. These may be summarized as follows:

1. The "directed" system, a *target* or *recipient* group, people who, whether they have asked for it or not, are the objects of a program whose goal is change in some aspect or aspects of their traditional way of life.

2. The "directing" system, an *innovating organization*, a bureaucracy, created, budgeted, and staffed with the personnel believed appropriate to achieve the goals deemed desirable — goals that represent change in the behavior of members of the target group.

3. The *interaction setting*, the point of contact, generally a specific, physical place, where the change agents of the innovating organization come into contact with the members of the target group, usually setting in motion a series of processes which result in greater or lesser change in the behavior forms of the latter. (Changes in the innovating organization may also result, although these are apt to be less marked.)

These topics, in the above order, are the substance of the following three chapters.

CHAPTER 4   the target group

THE RECIPIENT PEOPLES

When an anthropologist is hired to work in a directed culture change program, he is likely to turn his attention first to the target group. This may be a natural community, such as a Mexican or African village receiving help in community development, or it may be an organized or unorganized segment of a larger and more complex community, such as a hospital, a school, or the people of a neighborhood who can be attracted to an adult education program. For an agricultural extension service, the target is the farmers of a community or a county, while for a public health center, the target is that part of the surrounding population conforming to specific socioeconomic and other criteria.

Whether the target group is a genuine community or a more amorphous body, the initial research role of the anthropologist is to find out as much as possible about its culture and society. This means learning the social structure of the people, the ways in which their lives articulate within the family, within friendship and neighborhood networks, and within political and leadership

73

institutions. It means coming to understand the things people hold sacred, the values that have positive meaning to them. Above all, it means finding out how they think and reason, learning the bases for their logic, and fathoming the premises that underlie their behavior and determine their responses to new ideas and opportunities.

In studying a target group an anthropologist usually is quite at home; he is doing the research with which he is most familiar. In all probability he offered a community study in fulfillment of the dissertation requirement for his doctoral degree. He knows the problems of this kind of research, and he approaches them with confidence. He has demonstrated his ability to gain the confidence of similar groups and to establish rapport with informants. He knows how to begin his work and the paths he must travel to build a corpus of data and hypotheses that will permit interpretation of the people's way of life.

In an applied assignment an anthropologist quite naturally will place special emphasis on those aspects of culture — health beliefs and practices, agricultural methods, educational systems — that are the focus of interest of the innovating organization. In some instances, if the basic culture of the people is already well known, the anthropologist can go directly to such special topics. This was true in the analyses of health programs carried out by Institute of Social Anthropology personnel, briefly described in Chapter 1. The most rapid and effective studies of special problems of target groups can be done when the groundwork has already been laid. This is the most important argument for the support of general social anthropological research by action agencies. Such groundwork provides scientific capital, a resource that can be used in a great many ways. Institute of Social Anthropology personnel, with their excellent general knowledge of Latin American culture, could have worked equally well and rapidly on agricultural, educational, or community development projects.

With the ends of the innovating organization in mind, the ways in which an anthropologist can look at his research task are almost infinite. Simply as a device for coming to grips as rapidly as possible with new problem areas, in my own work as an applied anthropologist, I have found it helpful to organize my thinking around three major points: (1) the implications of cultural integration; (2) the explicit and implicit assumptions that underlie the customs and behavior of the group studied; (3) roles, and appraisals of role performance, by the people concerned. Each of these points will be examined in turn.

THE IMPLICATIONS OF CULTURAL INTEGRATION

It is axiomatic to anthropologists that each culture is a functional, integrated, internally consistent system, and not just a haphazard assemblage of customs and habits. Each part of a culture fulfills definite functions, supporting many other parts, and, in turn, drawing upon still others for its own functioning and well-being. To say that a culture is integrated does not, however, imply that its parts maintain perfect harmony and absolute balance. If this were so, a culture would be static and unchanging, a state that never exists in reality. In every culture, change occurs continually, although at vastly differing rates, so the elements of a culture are always in process of dislocation, and the struggle for their accommodation to each other goes on continually. In this struggle old elements drop out and new ones intrude; this substitution is essential for cultural viability. Hence, a culture, at any point in time, is always a compromise between stabilizing and dynamic forces; it is a system in a state of tension, of dynamic equilibrium, rather than of static repose.

A culture undergoing rapid change is under greater stress, and is more volatile, than one undergoing slower change. More old elements are disappearing, more new ones are entering, and, because a comfortable accommodation among elements requires time to effect, integration is less complete. Rapidly changing societies can, of course, be explosive places in which to try to bring about orderly change. But often, if lack of integration is not too extreme and life is not too uncertain, they offer unusual opportunities. As systems, they are less rigid, and hence more receptive to innovation, than are relatively static systems, which tend to build a hard shell of resistance around themselves, thus making penetration of novelty more difficult.

An appreciation of the implications of the functional, integrated nature of cultural systems is the key to successful directed change. The basic point is, of course, that *no change can occur in isolation.* Any change requires accommodations in the elements that most directly impinge upon the changing trait; if these accommodations cannot be made, the change will not occur. Conversely, any change is bound to produce secondary and tertiary changes. Sometimes these conditional changes are beneficial to a society, but sometimes they are prejudicial. The lesson to remember is that a single proposed change, such as may be considered by a change agent in planning for health, agriculture, or education, can never be evaluated solely in its own terms. It must be evaluated with regard to *all the other changes likely to occur* if it is successfully carried out. Only if, on balance, the total change picture offers more positive than negative perspectives, is a change agent justified in promoting a particular program.

To provide as broad a base as possible for evaluation of a proposed program, the basic technique of the applied anthropologist is to attempt to determine the relationship between the institutions or elements central to a proposed change, and the total cultural pattern. That is, he tries to identify the points where, say, health, educational, or agricultural practices articulate with the rest of society. After determining what appear to be the critical points, he asks what is likely to happen at each if a suggested program is implemented. To do this, he draws upon his knowledge of basic processes of cultural change which, worked out over time by means of the comparative method, allows him to make predictions in a general way in a wide variety of situations.

Health clinics are proposed in a rural area. The plan seems excellent, but what effect will it have, and what elements may inhibit its acceptance? The anthropologist knows that when vested interests are threatened, innovation will be opposed by these interests. What will be the attitude of traditional folk curers? Probably they will oppose the change. But the anthropologist knows that often folk curers and midwives have been made allies, rather than enemies, of modern medicine by assigning them formal status, giving them limited training, and making use of their undeniable abilities. The people to be served are very poor. Can they be attracted by free services? The anthropologist has learned most people are suspicious of free things. Experience has shown that, even for very poor people, a token price bestows value on goods or services, thus increasing the likelihood of acceptance. As we have seen, peoples with little exposure to scientific medicine often dichotomize illnesses: some, they recognize, can be treated successfully by medical doctors, while others, such as the evil eye, fright, witchcraft, and the like, are unknown to doctors and best treated by traditional means. The anthropologist knows that, if doctors and nurses working with traditional peoples are familiar with their ideas of folk medicine and can discuss illness in their own terms, they are more successful in gaining confidence — and patients — than if they deny such illnesses. These are some of the points an applied anthropologist would consider if assigned to work on a rural health program.

Primary Schools in Africa. In newly independent African countries, great emphasis is placed on primary education in rural areas. What factors bear upon success or failure? What conditions must prevail if a program is to be successful, and what conditions may severely handicap a program? Is the problem primarily financial: to be able to build schools and hire teachers? Obviously it is much more complex. Using local materials and local building techniques, adequate if not elegant structures can be built at low cost. Teachers' salaries are also low. But where are teachers found? Teacher training schools are a prerequisite to a village school system, and these institutions by necessity are more elaborate and costly to build, to operate, and to staff with well prepared teachers than the primary system they serve. Teacher training schools, teachers, and village schools thus require a national economy sufficiently productive to support them.

Even when these requirements are met, the problem is not

solved. Once exposed to the excitement of a city, an African youth
is reluctant to return as a teacher to an isolated village such as the
one in which, in all probability, he was raised. Ways must be found
to keep him happy in rural areas — perhaps by incentive pay and
frequent holidays and trips to cities. These devices, in turn, require
roads, good bus service, and fares low enough for him to afford.
Only when some such combination of conditions can be created
is there a reasonable chance of establishing a good village school
system.

A new school where none previously existed produces a re-
orientation in village ideas and in social and economic forms. In
Africa young children have great economic value as cattle tenders,
runners of errands, and general helpers. Their parents feel handicapped if they lose this support during most of the day. School
children may also require financial outlays for books, notebooks,
pencils, and perhaps better clothing than that previously worn.
Changes in the authority structure of the community also occur,
for parents must relinquish some control to another adult, the
teacher, and this may cause conflict. The role of teacher, previously
lacking, must be incorporated into the village social structure if
a school is to succeed.

Finally, what happens to children who complete a village school
curriculum? They are little or no better prepared for traditional
adult duties than children without schooling. A secondary education is essential if they are to make the contribution to their
country's development that is expected from an improved educational system. Secondary education is much more costly than primary education, so for a number of years relatively few primary
graduates will have the opportunity to continue their studies, a
fact which discourages both parents and village youth. It is of
slight value to awaken educational aspirations if these aspirations
cannot be satisfied. So what seems a relatively simple innovation
— village primary schools — must be seen as an immensely complex one, with a multitude of ramifications not apparent at first
thought.

ENVIRONMENTAL RESTRICTIONS

In addition to analyzing the prerequisites for and the probable results of a proposed innovation in terms of the integration of the cultural system itself, an applied anthropologist must consider the way in which the community is tied to its environment. Every environment offers potential for exploitation, and a major task of program planners is to identify existing opportunities. Irrigation, conservation, roads, and industry utilizing local resources are examples of exploitation of environmental possibilities. But environments also contain threats to well-being, or set limits to development and progress, which may override a planner's proposals. So in considering the possible implications of a proposed change, an anthropologist is concerned not only with social and cultural articulations, but also with the wider context of environment and ecology. The different ways in which an environment's opportunities and threats may bear upon planned change can be illustrated by two examples of the actual and potential consequences of irrigation projects in developing countries.

The Case of Bilharziasis. The agriculturalist and the economist correctly see irrigation as a major step forward in raising agricultural production of food and fibre to meet the needs of a growing world population. In Mexico, for example, major irrigation projects during the past two decades have turned the country from a food importing to a food exporting nation in spite of a near doubling of population. But in countries such as Egypt, the Sudan, and much of the remainder of Africa, in the Eastern Mediterranean, in Iraq, China, Japan, the Philippines, and Brazil, the disease *bilharziasis* (or *schistosomiasis*) gravely prejudices irrigation works. It is believed that in these countries as many as 150,000,000 people are infected. Several species of parasite of the genus *Schistosoma* are carried in infested water in a larval form which attaches itself to the skin of anyone who comes in contact with the water. The larva works through the skin and into the bloodstream, which carries it to the liver where it matures and mates. Eggs are laid in the walls of the intestines or bladder and then are excreted. Eggs reaching water hatch into free-swimming larvae that have a few hours to find a snail, which serves as host for the next cycle, which again leads back to man.

The disease rarely kills, but it weakens people so that they are easy prey to other illnesses. The cure is extended and painful, often obliging the patient to miss several weeks of work which usually he can ill afford. And without changes in the environment he will be quickly reinfected. Since contact with infested water is the source of the illness, any action which increases the amount of stagnant or slowly flowing water in which the snail hosts establish themselves, and which requires humans to spend much time in this water (as in transplanting irrigated rice), favors the spread of the disease. A World Health Organization report says, "In the Gezira part of the Sudan [the site of a particularly successful cotton growing scheme] . . . bilharziasis was occasionally found before the irrigation canals were built. Afterwards examinations showed that up to 80% of the children were infected. . . . During the last century the expansion of perennial irrigation in Egypt by storing the flood waters of the Nile has so fostered bilharziasis that it is now the most serious and the most expensive health problem of that country" (Anonymous 1963). Because of the ubiquity of this disease, it is estimated that economic productivity is reduced by 30 per cent in Egypt. The report concludes "it is possible that in some parts of the world the ravages of bilharziasis far outweigh the benefits of the urgently needed water brought by new irrigation dams." This is a heavy penalty to pay for more crop production, and in areas where the snail host occurs such programs can be considered successful only when means to eliminate the snail, and hence the disease, can be found.

Lake Pátzcuaro Irrigation. In the case of bilharziasis, the probable health consequence of irrigation works in areas where the host snail flourishes are now well recognized. The problem is not to predict; it is to find a way to eliminate the snail. But the same kind of close relationship between culture and environment exists in many places in different forms, and all planners are not yet alerted to the importance of considering ecology as a major and often critical factor in the success of their programs. Proposed irrigation works around Lake Pátzcuaro, in central Mexico, illustrate other dangers that lie in wait for the unwary.

Lake Pátzcuaro lies at an elevation of 7,000 feet and, surrounded by high mountains, it is the heart of one of the most beautiful parts of the country. Moreover, the villages surrounding the lake are picturesque, they produce a wide variety of arts and crafts, and the local markets, attended by Tarascan Indians as well as mestizos, are famous for their color and interest. The environmental characteristics that make the Pátzcuaro area attractive to tourists also limit its agricultural potential; except for relatively restricted but very fertile fields on the lake shore, agriculture is not productive, nor can it ever be made productive by comparison with other more richly endowed parts of the country. Natural resources are few, and the geographical relationships of the area with respect to big cities and major markets do not favor industrialization. In short, the one great economic potential of the region is tourism, at present only moderately exploited. Obviously preservation and enhancement of the attractions described are essential to the growth of this industry.

During recent years a number of planners, including several Americans, have proposed irrigating lake shore fields, and small pilot projects, with pumps, have been tried out. Although rain is abundant in Pátzcuaro, it does not always fall at critical times, so irrigation undoubtedly would improve crop yields. Under other circumstances no one could quarrel with irrigation proposals.

But let us examine more closely the geographical characteristics of the region. Lake Pátzcuaro lies at the bottom of an enclosed basin, with no outlet. The only water that reaches the lake comes from rain and runoff from the surrounding mountains, plus a few springs themselves dependent on the same water source. Unfortunately the total moisture available is inadequate to maintain historic lake levels, and over the years the trend is toward desiccation. The lake is now appreciably lower than in 1940, at which time in turn it was lower than in 1900. This gradual lowering of the lake has given farmers along the shore new areas of excellent land, but it also has adversely affected the livelihood of hundreds of Tarascan fishermen. And a drying lake would seriously jeopardize the tourist industry as well.

Those who recommend irrigation fail to recognize that *any* water drawn from within the drainage basin of the lake, whether impounded runoff or pumped directly from the lake, would significantly increase evaporation, thus hastening the drying of the lake. Although a few farmers would benefit, Tarascan fishermen would lose their livelihood, and the tourist attractions of the region would be gravely threatened. This technological "improvement," narrowly conceived and without thought to an ecological balance, can if carried out wreak havoc for the economy and welfare of the area in general.

THE ASSUMPTIONS UNDERLYING CUSTOM AND BEHAVIOR

The explicit and implicit assumptions that characterize the cognitive orientation of recipient peoples in a directed culture change program will have a major influence on their ability or inability, their willingness or unwillingness, to change traditional behavior and to respond positively to wisely conceived projects. In the traditional peasant world one of the most common and critical premises appears to be what I have called the "image of limited good" (Foster 1965, 1967a). It is an instance of what game theorists call the "zero sum game" situation, which predicts behavior when resources are limited.

The Limited Good Premise. This premise and the ways in which it affects peasant behavior are most easily understood in contrast to the "unlimited good" premise that prevails among members of the middle and upper classes of industrialized countries. In the United States, most members of these classes take it for granted that science, technology, and managerial talents, rationally coordinated with the exploitation of natural resources, will produce growth rates in output of goods and services that exceed population growth rates. This means that with each passing generation people on average will have more of the good things in life than did their predecessors. An important corollary of the unlimited good premise is that there is ample "room at the top," that the success of one person does not mean denial or loss for another, except perhaps in rather specialized instances — say, the presidency of the country. Even in industry, where the same zero sum game rules sometimes seem to hold, a man denied the presidency of his firm may move to the same position in a rival company. This view of economic opportunity and the good life produces an optimism about the future, a willingness to take chances, to try new ways. It is a dynamic force promoting change and progress.

In contrast, in societies where economic systems are essentially static, or are still thought to be static even in the face of contemporary improvements, where by extension of this view *all* desired things in life are assumed to exist in finite and unexpandable quantities, people's ideas about change and progress are quite different. If the economic pie and the corollary pies of all other good things are seen as constants within a community, it follows that an advancement in the standard of living for one person can come only at the expense of others. A villager who rises in some way — who acquires better clothing, improves his house, or perhaps buys a radio — is immediately suspect in a traditional community, for his fellows find it hard to believe that he has created or produced more and is simply enjoying the fruits of this increased production. In peasant societies and among other underprivileged peoples, innovative people tend to be seen as rapacious and greedy. Because they are upsetting the traditional distribution of "good," of the limited resources of the group, they are viewed as threats to community stability rather than as entrepreneurial models to be emulated. For this reason they frequently are criticized, slandered, and condemned in the hope that this will discourage what is seen as antisocial behavior. Unfortunately, these negative sanctions often discourage the very individuals capable of leading the way into the modern world.

In the traditional peasant world (i.e., depending on place, peasant villages as they functioned until about a generation ago), this view of reality was not far from accurate. Peasants were (and are) poor, their production was low, and they enjoyed few of the medical, educational, welfare, and other advantages taken for granted by more fortunate people. But since World War II developmental activities have brought new opportunities and possibilities to growing numbers of peasants. Increasingly they are taking advantage of these new situations. Nevertheless there is always a cognitive lag, and the realization that one can progress without threatening others comes more slowly than the opportunity itself. In Tzintzuntzan, for example, a small number of families — perhaps twenty — have passed a critical cultural threshold: they realize the new possibilities, work hard to take advantage of them, compete for prestige (with such things as gas stoves and television), and worry less and less about their still critical, more conservative neighbors. These people, and others like them in similar communities, are the ones who set the new pace of progress. But if the traditional image of limited good could be swept away overnight and be replaced by an awareness of contemporary reality and its opportunities, progress would come to Tzintzuntzan far more rapidly.

In industrial countries people assume that they have significant mastery over their environments and are able to bring about major improvements in their physical surroundings as well as in their social conditions. This idea, of course, underlies all planning, including directed culture change programs. But these assumptions about the possibilities of improvement and progress are not universals in all human minds. Beals describes how, in the traditional Indian peasant community of Gopalpur, people do not regard prevailing patterns "as something to be changed, improved, or fought. Things, both good and bad, are as they always have been and as they always will be" (Beals 1962:11). Obviously for people with such a cognitive orientation, a change agent's first job is not simply to present innovation possibilities: it is to try to crack this wall of fatalism and find ways to modify prevailing outlooks.

Science Education in Nepal. How an implicit assumption about knowledge presents problems for a new educational approach is illustrated by data from Nepal. In that country a joint Nepalese-American effort is being made to introduce the teaching of contemporary science in traditional schools. At first glance this would appear to require only translation of standard texts, perhaps substitution of examples based on Nepalese life and conditions rather than on those of the United States, and the acquisition of simple laboratory equipment for demonstration and experiment. Implicit in the American approach is the assumption that knowledge is infinite and that discovery of new knowledge knows no end. Hence education should be designed to encourage enquiring, questioning, experimental minds.

But the basic assumption underlying knowledge in Nepal is diametrically opposed to this view. There, the traditional view is that *all knowledge is already known*, that nothing remains to be discovered. ". . . The predominant view is one that pictures human knowledge about nature as a closed body, rarely if ever capable of extension, which is passed down from teacher to student and from generation to generation. Its source is authority, not observation" (Dart and Pradhan 1967:652). As a function of this premise, education based on rote learning — the traditional Nepalese method — makes complete sense. The imaginative scholar searches out a guru with the knowledge he wishes to acquire and then attempts to memorize this knowledge. Obviously, in designing a science education curriculum for Nepalese schools, as Dart and Pradhan are doing, the planners must be aware of *their own* fundamental assumptions about knowledge, and of how these differ from those of the target group. Only then can a reasonable educational program be drawn up.

VIEWS OF ROLE PERFORMANCE

The views people hold about the nature and quality of role performance have a great deal to do with the acceptance or rejection of innovation. People like to feel they are "needed" in their families, in their communities, or in their professional or occupational groups, and that they competently perform tasks that have importance. They derive satisfaction and security from the conviction that the roles they have chosen, or which society has thrust upon them, are necessary and worthwhile, and that they fulfill them ably. Any act, event, or innovation that ridicules their roles, that suggests they are unimportant, or that they do not fulfill them satisfactorily, is thus viewed with alarm. (As we saw in Chapter 1, Venezuelan mothers interpreted free powdered milk for their infants as a reflection on their ability to provide rich and abundant milk from their own breasts.)

Threats to a person's self-image, to his belief that he ably fulfills important roles, obviously will be repelled. Often new projects or innovations run afoul of this kind of resistance because the change agent is unaware of the significance of role performance and of how his project may affect traditional views of such performance. To illustrate, when instant coffee was first introduced in the United States it met with resistance from many housewives. Early advertising stressed the time-saving element, but this proved relatively unsuccessful. Research revealed that many housewives felt the ability to make good coffee was an element of prestige in the homemaker's role, and that they derived much satisfaction from the recognition that they did this well. " 'Time-saving' therefore was regarded by many women householders as containing an implicit suggestion that the duty of preparing coffee was perhaps inessential or unimportant, or that their skill was unequal to their position in the household" (Wilson 1962:4–5). Subsequent advertising stressed the excellence of flavor of powdered coffee rather than the time-saving element.

Wilson points out further that "In most societies women have a multiple role — of household manager, of mother and of wife. In commercial practice, it is important to recognize that the basis on which a woman will judge a new product will depend on the particular role in which she regards herself at the time of considering it; and on which role is stressed in making an approach to her in the marketing and advertising policy on the product concerned" (ibid., 5). These remarks apply equally to the presentation of new ideas to target group members. Innovations that strengthen traditional roles or at least do not threaten them are more likely to be accepted than those which threaten a role. A public health nurse in an international program in Taiwan preferred half-polished rice for its nutritional value over the more prestigious polished rice. Her cook, however, felt that to be asked to prepare low class food cast reflections on her role and her cooking ability. She therefore, without asking permission, substituted her own polished rice for the less prestigious rice of her employer (communicated by Merle S. Farland, R.N.).

The use of improved seeds is a major element in many agricultural programs. Opler and Singh tell how in the village they studied in India the government provided good seed at a fair price, well within the means of a great many of the farmers. Strangely, the wealthiest and most able farmers were most resistant to the improved strains. "It has long been thought a disgrace and a sign of failure or poor management to be forced to borrow or buy seed. The village farmer takes special pride in being able to raise enough food to maintain his family and in having enough left over to use as seed. . ." (Opler and Singh 1952:7). Hence, to suggest that the best agriculturalists buy seed was tantamount to telling them that they were not competently filling their role as farmers.

Village schools in Ethiopia have encountered difficulties because parents, especially fathers, feel threatened in their role as teachers of correct behavior and manners. At school the child is encouraged to participate in discussion, to ask questions, and to take responsibility and develop a sense of leadership. This directly contravenes established custom. At home the child is told he is still young, and he is criticized for having new ideas and for expressing them. The new school behavior carries the implication that the role of parent is not being properly filled in the home (communicated by Lemma Menouta).

In many parts of the world new maternal and child health clinics pose a threat to the older women in the family who, traditionally, are concerned with guiding a mother through pregnancy, with delivery of the infant, and with the care of the child. Not surprisingly, to have outsiders (who may be young and perhaps unmarried women) assert greater knowledge about these traditional roles

88

is viewed as a great threat. The older women are being told, in effect, that they are not able to fill a role they had always assumed to be of great importance, and for which they believed they were well prepared by experience and age. Where familial authority remains strong, older women sometimes prevent young mothers from utilizing maternal and child health clinics.

Role perception and views are important to directed change programs in another way. Just as an innovation that suggests a role is unimportant, or that the incumbent fills it badly, is received with scant enthusiasm, so too is an innovation that puts a person in a role seemingly inappropriate to his age, sex, occupation, and general station in life. Adult education programs in developing countries often are handicapped because the role of student is associated with children and not with adults. To suggest that an adult assume the role of a child, even temporarily, implies that the change agent does not fully appreciate the adult's dignity and worth. In Northern Rhodesia in 1962 the extension of peanut farming, which was being pushed by the agricultural department, was slowed because of role conflicts. Peanuts had long been grown for domestic consumption, but their cultivation was considered to be women's work. Initially African farmers were reluctant to assume a woman's role (author's field notes).

In the early days of the Indian community development program, compost pits were dug on the outskirts of a number of villages for the deposit of cattle manure and refuse. Role conflict, however, prevented full utilization of these pits. Traditionally women clean cattle stables, and even those of the highest castes can do this inside the walls of their homes. But women of higher castes could not be seen carrying such refuse in public places. Men also refused to transport manure because, as with peanut farming in Africa, it was part of the task of women, and so to undertake a woman's job was seen as a threat to male dignity (Dube 1956: 21-22).

CONCLUSIONS

As an applied anthropologist comes to understand the ways in which the society he is studying is integrated, as he learns the premises on which behavior is based, and as he appreciates the meaning and nature of role performances, he becomes increasingly useful to the planners, administrators, and technical experts with whom he is associated. He explains what he has learned, discusses with them the feasibility of alternate approaches, and analyzes the probable consequences of decisions. He helps them plan projects which do minimum violence to customary ways and which, where-ever possible, build on preexisting forms. When he is convinced that recommended new practices represent genuine improve-ments, and not just a planner's dream of what should be, he helps change agents to develop strategies for presenting projects so that recipient peoples will be motivated to change, so that they will perceive advantage in giving up old ways and in adopting new ones. And, as we will see in the following chapter, at the same time the anthropologist is studying the innovating organization to which his change agent colleagues belong, so that he can explain to them how *their* social and cultural forms affect their performance.

CHAPTER 5   the innovating
                             organization

THREE STAGES OF AWARENESS

In earlier years colonial administrators, and program planners and technical specialists in developmental projects, assumed that the "human" problems on which anthropologists could shed light were rooted in the cultures of dependent peoples or target groups. Anthropologists shared this opinion. Consequently, for a great many years applied anthropological research differed little if at all from traditional research. The principal objects of attention, in most instances, were native peoples or members of recipient groups toward whom health, agricultural, or educational programs were being directed.

Today we are beginning to realize that knowledge about the social and cultural forms of the innovating organization, about the structure and functions of bureaucratic institutions, is just as essential as knowledge about recipient peoples to successful planned change. This recognition has come late, and many people still fail to appreciate it. For this reason anthropologists have made few studies of innovating organizations in the context of their effectiveness in achieving stated goals. Rather, we must turn to sociology for case studies of bureaucracies and for general theory about bureaucracy.* Few of these studies, however, bear directly upon how administrative cultures facilitate or inhibit directed change among target peoples, so this is one of the areas in which anthropological research is most needed.

To appreciate why it is important to the success of directed change programs to study administrative cultures, it is necessary to outline three phases of growing awareness of the complexity of the nontechnical factors that bear on development and progress. These may be described as follows.

Application of Preexisting Techniques. When planners and technical specialists first became concerned with the intercultural transfer of scientific technology in fields such as medicine, agriculture, and education, almost without exception their assumptions about the nature of the problem were highly ethnocentric: identify a problem, and attack it with the most advanced techniques used in the technologically developed countries (which of course supplied the planners and technical experts). Two main assumptions were involved. The first was that people in underdeveloped areas immediately appreciate the advantage of new ways, once exposed to them, and that given the opportunity they will quickly adopt them. The second was that the best and most advanced technologies work just as well in underdeveloped areas as in the highly developed countries which produced them. The following example illustrates these assumptions.

Anti-Hookworm Work in Ceylon. At the beginning of the Rockefeller Foundation anti-hookworm campaign, carried out in Ceylon from 1916 to 1922, it was assumed that an intensive campaign in a pilot area would wipe out the disease and demonstrate both the need for and the methods of eliminating hookworm from the island. The program included a census, sanitary surveys to locate

* No value judgment is implied in the use of the word "bureaucracy." In my usage I follow Blau, who describes bureaucracy as "The type of organization designed to accomplish large-scale administrative tasks by systematically coordinating the work of many individuals . . ." (Blau 1967:14).

sources of infection, installation of latrines, microscopic examination of feces of everyone in the trial area, and treatment of infected persons. This approach, when tried in the American South, had worked well. But it was far from successful in Ceylon. The target population, docile at first, became actively hostile and uncooperative, and tea plantation managers often opposed the experiment because treatment of laborers caused the loss of many working days. The complaints of the workers themselves were numerous, and not the least was that hookworm was by no means the most important of their health problems. The program eventually achieved considerable success, but not before the initial approach had been greatly broadened by relating hookworm control more closely to other health programs. Subsequent analysis of this early experiment has shown that "The problems of parasites, nutrition, sanitation, social conditions, and economics are interlocked. An improvement in any one of these areas of human problems will affect one or more of the others. But at the same time a lack of improvement in one of the areas may hold back progress in all the others. An invaluable byproduct of the Rockefeller hookworm work was the demonstration that no pertinent gain can be made in combating disease without a general rise in the social and economic level" (Philips 1955:302).

In spite of lessons like this, when the United States government embarked upon its first major technical aid programs in Latin America in 1942 the same philosophy prevailed: take as models American programs, duplicate them as nearly as possible in the host country, and they will meet the local needs. It was assumed that the advantages of complex and sophisticated programs were self-evident. As with the hookworm campaign, the naïveté of this assumption quickly became apparent. It was realized that a program evolved according to the needs of a technologically advanced country cannot simply be grafted onto the structure of a country with different needs and different social and cultural forms.

Analysis of the Recipient Group Culture. The early ethnocentric view of technical aid gave way to a stage — continuing to the present time, and still thought by many to be the sophisticated view of the problem — that can be called "anthropological." According to this view, the major problems in technological development are imbedded in the society and culture of the community itself. Recipient peoples, it is assumed, are basically anxious to raise their standards of living and are willing to modify their behavior under certain circumstances. But psychological, social, and cultural barriers inhibit these changes. Consequently, if these barriers can be identified through intensive study of the community, and if the motivations to change that exist can be discovered, then programs can be presented in such a way that client peoples will adopt them eagerly. This is the "In order to achieve success in directed culture change it is essential to know the target group's culture" stage. The case histories in Chapter 1 reflect this point of view, for their emphasis is on understanding the social, economic, political, and religious systems of recipient peoples, and the values relevant to each system. In colonial administration, with emphasis on Indirect Rule, applied anthropology advanced very little beyond this approach. Even today a good many anthropologists see it as representing the focus of applied work. The point of view is not in itself wrong. It *is* essential to understand the way of life of the members of a target group in order to plan and execute the most effective programs. But we must go further; we must consider *all* the significant factors. Often, however, this point of view has been adequate for limited goals, as the following illustration demonstrates.

Smallpox Vaccination in Papua. About 1914 the native peoples of Papua (a part of New Guinea) were threatened by smallpox. Hubert Murray, the lieutenant governor, was endowed with an innate sense of the significance of cultural differences, and he reacted to the situation in a way unusual at the time. Since he felt that forcible vaccination would not achieve his ends, he resorted to an indirect method. "We told them that there was a very dangerous and powerful sorcerer . . . and that this sorcerer had conjured up a very bad sickness which might come along at any moment. But, though the sorcerer was strong, the Government was stronger, and would protect all who claimed its protection. A mark would be put on the arm of all those who trusted themselves to the Government; the sorcerer when he came would see the Government mark, would realize that he was powerless, and would retire foiled and baffled. . . . But for those who would not receive the mark the Government could, of course, do nothing." The plan was sensationally successful; the government mark became socially popular "and to be without the mark was to confess oneself the veriest outsider" (Murray 1921:167).

Analysis of the Innovating Organization's Culture. As sophistication in identifying directed culture change problems has grown, it has become apparent that knowledge of the "culture" of the innovating organization is just as important as knowledge of the target group. Just as barriers to change are found in cultural forms in peasant villages, they are found in the structure and values and operating procedures of bureaucracies, and in the personal qualities of the change agents. In contemporary developmental work these barriers constitute grave problems, partly because their significance is not yet fully appreciated and partly because most administrative organizations are even more rigid and more resistant to change than peasant villagers and other client peoples. Sophisticated technical aid specialists increasingly feel that the frequently monolithic character of bureaucracy constitutes the biggest problem in perfecting the techniques of directed change planning and operation. Ways must be found for such organizations to understand themselves, and to change to meet contemporary problems. For this reason, detailed behavioral science analysis of organizations engaged in directed culture change is slowly being recognized as just as important to the anthropologist's task as analysis of the target group. This is the "In order to achieve success in directed culture change it is essential to know the innovating bureaucracy's culture" stage. In this chapter attention is directed to this point, the study of the characteristics of innovating organizations, and the ways in which these characteristics influence change.

BUREAUCRACIES AS SOCIAL
AND CULTURAL SYSTEMS

A bureaucracy in its structural and dynamic aspects is strikingly like a "natural" community such as a tribe or peasant village. It is a real society with a real culture. Normally it is composed of people of both sexes and of different ages, organized in a hierarchy of authority, responsibility, obligations, and functional tasks. It thus has a social structure which defines the relationships, roles, and statuses of all the members of the group with respect to each other. Through recruitment (rather than birth), it continually brings new members into the system, thus ensuring viability and continuity. Through formal and informal educational methods, it teaches the role behavior expected of new members, as well as the values, routines, and premises of the organization. And through retirement and the ritual of testimonial dinners (rather than death rites), it terminates membership when a person is no longer deemed competent to fulfill his role.

A bureaucracy further resembles a natural community in that it is an integrated, functional unit in which the parts fit together, if not with perfect consistency at least well enough to make it viable. Too viable, at times: nothing is harder to kill off than a bureaucracy whose reason for existing has disappeared. And, as with natural communities, no change in a bureaucracy comes about in isolation, without rearrangement in the role relationships of its members, without increasing the responsibility and authority of some and diminishing that of others. Like people in natural communities, bureaucrats jealously guard their traditional perquisites and privileges; they do not easily surrender their vested interests, except in exchange for something as good or better. They rationalize their positions by assuring themselves that what is good for them is best for their organization.

Bureaucracies are similar to natural societies in another way: within the norms of behavior and values that characterize both, individual members exhibit great variation in character and personality, views and judgments. All people have varied and complex relationships with others in their societies and, when they work in directed change programs, with people in other societies as well. People are not simply carriers of cultures; they are also psychological entities with the need to receive ego gratification and satisfaction from what they do. They are characterized by emotional securities and insecurities, likes and dislikes, doubts and hopes. Sometimes they feel highly successful in their accomplishments; at other times they may feel threatened or rejected, the objects of unjustified aggression.

Finally, bureaucratic "cultures" are similar to other cultures in that they are based on explicit and implicit premises to which their members subscribe and which they take for granted. Actually, in an administrative structure we can identify three levels of premises: (1) general, national premises that bureaucrats share with the other members of their societies; (2) premises which are not specific to any profession, but which characterize bureaucracies per se; (3) premises specific to a profession, and to a bureaucracy based on this profession. At all three levels the prevailing premises will profoundly influence program planning and execution.

National Premises. American bureaucrats, largely recruited from middle class society, share the same basic premises as American professional people, as businessmen, as university professors, and as others with the same background and educational experience. Some of these premises are: an expanding economy offers greater opportunity to all, and one person's success does not jeopardize another's opportunities; competent people appear in all socioeconomic strata, and not just in the economically privileged classes, so that the Good Society is the one that maximizes the possibilities of educating and utilizing such people; economic values override other values, and the measure of any proposal is "does it make sense economically?"; man has achieved mastery over nature, and expects to control it in extensive degree; the basic problems of the world are technological and, given enough money and manpower, they can be solved; life is not tragic, and a "happy ending" is everyone's right; hard work is a value in itself, and prolonged idleness is bad; if people aren't with us, they are against us. The list is illustrative rather than definitive. Premises such as these, which are common to millions of Americans, influence the views of bureaucrats and of program planners and administrators in directed change projects to an extent usually not recognized.

In Britain, in contrast, the premises of the upper classes (from which have come the policy-making civil servants) traditionally have been rather different. Among the major beliefs of this group are: very few really superior biological specimens are produced in any society; nature is stingy in turning out people competent to rule, to make decisions about the welfare of a nation, and to carry on its intellectual and scientific life; consequently, the Good Society must identify its superior people at an early age and give them the best possible education to prepare them for the responsibilities nature has thrust upon them; people like this are easily identifiable because over generations they have risen to the top, acquiring control over means of production, finance, higher education, and the established church; people in these positions naturally produce more of their kind, so that it is here the major selection is made.*

Members of the upper classes form The Establishment, a largely self-perpetuating society based on birth, breeding, accent, manners, the right public schools and universities, wealth, and a sense of community. Barbara Tuchman gives a good picture of Establishment premises prior to World War I: "Their credo was the exact opposite of the idea prevailing in the more newly minted United States, that there was a peculiar extra virtue in being lowly born, that only the self-made carried the badge of ability and that men of easy circumstances were more likely than not to be stupid or wicked, if not both. The English, on the contrary, having evolved slowly through generations of government by the possessing class, assumed that prolonged retention by one family of education, comfort and social responsibility was the natural nour-

---

* These are nineteenth- and early twentieth-century premises. Needless to say, in Britain since World War II they have been held by a smaller and smaller number of people.

ishment of 'superior fitness' " (Tuchman 1966:13). Obviously there is no "cult of the common man" here, no belief in the ability of the masses (especially the unschooled masses) to judge for themselves what is best for them.

The community development movement well illustrates the ways in which differing national premises influence the design and administration of programs, producing projects which theoretically conform to a common model but are in fact quite distinct.

Community Development and National Premises. Community development, especially in rural areas, has played an important part since World War II in the developmental plans of many nations. The basic philosophical principle underlying this kind of work is that the common man, however unschooled, possesses wisdom, and that with help he is capable of identifying his major needs and capable of helping to find answers to them. The community development worker's role is that of catalyst, to stimulate village people to meet, to discuss their problems and wants, to plan, and to take action. Knowing government resources, he is then able to channel such help as may be available into village projects. The qualities found in the best community development worker include the ability to consult with villagers, the patience necessary to hear them out, and a humility that permits him to learn from others. Where American middle class technical specialists have worked in community development programs they have, following their national premises, adhered in large measure to this philosophy.

In contrast, British colonial community development work in Northern Rhodesia (prior to its emergence as independent Zambia in 1964) consciously and unconsciously was based on traditional Establishment premises. Thus, it logically followed, especially in a colonial setting, that "superior" people (in this case, those who administered the colony) had not only the right but the duty to plan for and govern the common people in an autocratic fashion. As a consequence, community development in Northern Rhodesia took a form rather different from that found in many other countries. Policy-making officers and program administrators were detailed from the Ministry of Native Affairs, which was charged with the administration of all non-Europeans in the colony. These officers, of course, shared Establishment attitudes and conception of responsibilities. In their previous administrative and developmental activities they had assumed their task was to decide what needed doing, and then bend every effort to achieve the goals that were set. In their new assignments these same views prevailed. Having little faith in the African villager's ability to identify his needs and to articulate his wants and aspirations, they made little effort to discuss problems with people. They assumed that in village level community development, as in basic colonial administration, their task was to decide what would be good for people and for the country, and then to marshal their slim resources to attempt to achieve the goals they set for themselves. They tended to see the community development movement as a communication device, a way of persuading apathetic natives to do what the government felt was best for them.

Obviously the implicit premises of the members of the innovating organization (as well as the whole social structure of the colonial setting) produced a form of community development quite distinct from that found in most other countries. The intentions of the officers were good; they were men of high ideals and very considerable ability, and they were genuinely interested in the welfare of the natives. Yet their assumptions about ability and character, as well as their previous professional experience, made it almost impossible for them to comprehend or accept the community development philosophy (author's field notes).

Bureaucratic Premises. Below the level of national premises we find that of generalized bureaucratic premises, premises which are generic to bureaucracy as a system rather than to any particular type of organization. Perhaps the most pervasive of these premises is that size is important, that an administrative organization must grow continually in order to be healthy. This premise is a consequence of other premises. In most bureaucracies it is assumed that the importance of a position is determined by the number of people the incumbent supervises. Often salary increases can be obtained only when it is shown that an administrator directs more people and has more responsibility than when his rank was set. Naturally, the aggressive administrator will do everything possible to increase the size of his "operation," thus contributing to the expansion of his agency, whether or not such expansion is in fact in the best interests of the organization. Thus, bureaucracies usually see themselves in direct competition with many other bureaucracies, and in large organizations there is much jockeying and infighting to prevent reorganizations that may result in loss of functions or units to other offices or bureaus, however logical such changes may be. At the same time, the able official is alert to the possibilities of raiding some other organization, thus augmenting his importance and that of his unit.

A not infrequent premise of administrative systems, and until relatively recent times one characteristic of much American and British industry, is the "work your way up from the bottom" syndrome. According to this premise, in order to acquire the knowledge necessary for top level responsibility a young man must start at the bottom, work in as many departments or units as possible, and master in detail all operations. Only after years of varied experiences within an organization can he be expected to have the wisdom and knowledge necessary for executive authority. This philosophy, when strictly adhered to, finished off a good many once prosperous businesses, for it produced narrow, professionally ethnocentric executives who were masters of details but who often lacked knowledge of the broad picture and of the changes going on about them. Fresh ideas and new ways of looking at conventional problems are the qualities most needed by top administrators, yet these are the ones usually stultified by the "work your way up from the bottom" system.

The British colonial system also was based in significant degree on this premise. When I observed it in operation in Northern Rhodesia in 1962 almost no one questioned the view that it was possible to learn of and to be able to solve the problems inherent in colonial administration only by serving at all levels of the service, in many parts of the territory. One exceptional officer commented upon his surprise when, detailed to accompany a British parliamentary delegation spending several weeks in the territory, he found that people who knew how to ask the right questions could learn a great deal in a short time, and could point out serious flaws in standard operating procedures, as well as in the premises on which these procedures were based, which no one within the system had recognized.

A particularly common assumption in bureaucracies is that administrators at higher levels "know best," that by virtue of long experience within the system they are qualified to make plans and pass judgment on the widest variety of matters. Of course, the purpose of executive authority is to delegate broad responsibilities to individuals who have shown exceptional ability; such allocation of decision-making authority is essential for an organization to function. At the same time there is always danger that unquestioned authority may lead to complacency and to the assumption that the decision-maker knows all of the significant factors in the situation for which he is responsible. The two following examples illustrate how the easy acceptance of authority may work against rational change.

A Village Pilot Project in Mexico. In the 1950's the Mexican Ministry of Hacienda wished to demonstrate its conviction that standards of living in backward communities could be raised most economically by providing villages with *all* basic services and meeting *all* their needs simultaneously. This conviction, held by high ranking officials of a prestigious ministry, was at odds with the developmental philosophy of officials of the less prestigious National Indian Institute who, like other community developers, stressed involvement of the local people. To make its demonstration as striking as possible, Ministry of Hacienda personnel selected the poorest and most change resistant community they could find: Santo Tomás Chiautla, near Tehuacán, Puebla. The five hundred people of this village earn their meager living by taking stone from a nearby quarry to chip *metates* (maize-grinding stones) and mortars and pestles, which are sold over a wide area. Ministry economists offered the community, absolutely free, a school, a health center, a pharmacy, credit to buy jackhammers for quarrying stone, and other facilities. Far from gaining acceptance, the economists were run out of town. The Mexican anthropologist Héctor García Manzanedo, sent to investigate the cause of this strange behavior, was also ultimately forced to leave the village, but not before he found out the reason for the rejection of help. In a society lacking the concept of "gift," where all help and services are on a reciprocal, exchange basis, people could not believe one could receive something — and especially so much — without having to give something in return. The villagers suspected a catch, probably a clever government scheme to rob them of their quarry, the only thing of value they controlled (communicated by Dr. García). Had ministry planners been less convinced of their omniscience, and had they taken the trouble to learn something about village psychology, they would have presented their project in a different fashion, with greater chances of success.

Depth Charges in the British Navy. At the beginning of World War II the custom in the British Navy was to set depth charges (to destroy submerged enemy submarines) to explode at one hundred feet. The practice was a long standing one, based on the belief that at that depth, water pressure caused the detonation to have maximum power. The figure presumably had been decided upon by an admiral or board at an earlier, less scientific period in undersea warfare, and it had been accepted uncritically ever since. An outside research team assigned to study depth charge practices questioned the figure and, using probability theory, determined that a detonation depth of thirty-five feet would greatly increase the percentage of "kills." For the team to have its recommendations tried out "was no easy matter since they were striking at the roots of rules of action which were hallowed by years of tradition" (Eddison 1953:64). But the recommendations were given a "grudging trial," wonderfully vindicating the scientists when the increased number of sinkings reported corresponded almost exactly to the levels predicted. "Operational research [of which this is an example] is a challenge to established beliefs, customs and traditions," says Eddison; "it strikes at complacency" (*ibid.*, 65). The same is true of applied anthropological research directed to uncovering the premises that underlie conventional bureaucratic practices, and then questioning whether in fact these premises reflect the contemporary situation.

Professional Premises. Individual bureaucracies and the professional subcultures with which they are associated, such as medical, educational, legal, and welfare systems, also reflect the premises of the professionals who staff them. Doctors, nurses, agricultural experts, teachers, and community developers all exhibit professional behavior determined not only by the premises of their national society, and by those of bureaucracies per se, but also by premises unique to their professions. Medical people, for example, assume that life is sacred and that every effort must be made to preserve it, whatever the cost in time, money, medical skills, and perhaps overpopulation and human suffering. Agricultural experts believe that the highest possible yield per unit of land must be achieved, with the fewest possible farm hands. Educators are convinced that, given enough education, all the world's problems can be solved. Community developers often assume that goals achieved on any basis other than that of community cooperation are valueless. It is essential that an applied anthropologist fathom the premises of the professionals with whom he is working (and that he understand his own as well), if he is to understand the rationale for the programs with which he is associated and be able to evaluate them objectively.

Some of the ways in which professional assumptions influence development and change are well illustrated by the following examples of education in former British Africa.

Higher Education in British Africa. Eric Ashby, in a recent monumental analysis of the design and policy of British-directed higher education in India and Africa, points out how professional premises (to some extent coupled with national premises) produced universities not well suited to the needs of emerging nations. "Underlying British enterprise in providing higher education for her people overseas was one massive assumption: that the pattern of university appropriate for Manchester, Exeter and Hull was *ipso facto* appropriate for Ibadan, Kampala, and Singapore. . . . As with cars, so with universities: we willingly made minor modifications to suit the climate, but we proposed no radical change in design; and we did not regard it as our business to enquire whether French or American models might be more suitable" (Ashby 1966: 244). These assumptions were linked with another assumption, that the colonies would be under British rule at least for most of the rest of the twentieth century and that after independence the universities' ties with Britain would remain close. Ashby recognizes, as have other critics of the system, that the direct transplantation of British higher education resulted in universities less well suited to preparing Africans for independence and for the problems of their developing countries than would universities designed as functions of African conditions and needs. Just as the American land grant university grew up in response to needs quite different from those envisaged in traditional British higher education, so a new type of colonial university might better have served the needs of the countries concerned.

Primary Education in British Africa. By pointing out the unquestioned assumptions of primary school education in Britain, and by contrasting these assumptions to the reality of African life, Musgrove makes clear the conceptual chasm that separates English teachers from Ugandan students. "In England a teacher . . . merely elaborates and explains an already accepted culture; but among the tribes of Uganda he is justifying the novel notions of a new one. He himself may not always be aware of the assumptions he is making . . ." (Musgrove 1953:111). Since the cultural forces that have produced African logic are quite different from those producing English logic, students react very differently to common experiences: "They are not convinced of the fundamental assumption that events in nature and society happen in that way and for those reasons: they have not been persuaded of this pattern of causality. They will attribute a man's poverty either to his personal deficiencies, or, more probably, to the machinations of an enemy. But the effective causes of social circumstances are individual men, albeit, perhaps, exerting supernatural powers, operating through the essentially personal extension of magic" (*ibid.*, 115). And finally, whereas in England "a teacher illustrates truths, in Africa he must prove them. . . . *The teacher's first business is to be aware of the nature and assumptions of his own culture, and then to understand where and how it differs from that of his pupils* (*ibid.*, 116 — emphasis added).

CONTINUOUS-AIM FIRING IN THE AMERICAN NAVY

Before turning to the final theme of this chapter, that of the relationship between premises and innovation, I will attempt to recapitulate those topics already discussed through the classic example, analyzed by Morison, of "continuous-aim firing." In this illustration we see how the Navy bureaucracy is a specialized society characterized by its own culture, how its personnel jealously guard their privileges and perquisites, and how its structure and premises draw together to reject the threat of major changes, the consequences of which it cannot fully foresee or control.

In 1898 a British naval officer, Sir Percy Scott, invented a way of permitting naval rifles to remain trained on target in spite of the roll of the ship, which previously had been impossible. In 1900 Scott and a young American naval officer, Lieutenant (later Admiral) William S. Sims, met when both were stationed on the China Coast. From Scott, Sims learned about continuous-aim firing, recognized its great superiority, and immediately set about trying to introduce it into the American Navy. But the Navy bureaucracy conspired at every point to stifle Lieutenant Sims, and only when he appealed directly to President Theodore Roosevelt, and was given the authority necessary to force change, was he able to bring about this essential improvement, which increased firing accuracy by 6,000 per cent. The principal reasons for resistance, says Morison, were not that Sims was a junior officer 8,000 miles from Washington, nor that he was criticizing the men responsible for current practices, nor that existing methods were thought to be as good as any in the world. Rather, the most important reason was that "the Navy is not only an armed force: *it is a society*" (Morison 1950:9 — emphasis added). Not only is it a society but, like all military organizations, it is an extremely tight and rigid society whose prevailing forms and values, at the time of the incident, had been established during a period of relatively slow technological change. In the years following the Civil War, until the appearance of Lieutenant Sims, it had been pushed to its limits by the rapid technological developments that characterized this period. "To these numerous innovations, producing as they did a spreading disorder throughout a service with heavy commitments to formal organization, the Navy responded with grudging pain" (*ibid.*, 9). Continuous-aim firing doubtless seemed like the straw that would break the camel's back.

Morison sees the primary reason for resistance to this innovation as based on the military man's conscious and subconscious recognition that a change in technology presages a change in the forms of his society, and on his usual desire to maintain the structure of the society with which he has learned to live. When continuous-aim firing finally was introduced, it wrought great changes not only in ship design, shipboard routine, and fleet tactics, but also in social relationships. Gunnery officers, until this time of little importance, became extremely powerful members of a ship's company, and many were promoted more rapidly than and ahead of officers previously their superiors, to the discomfort and envy, quite naturally, of the latter (*ibid.*, 9–10).

PREMISES AND INNOVATION

As we have seen, the formal structure and the values of bureaucracies, the nature of the relationships among their functionaries, and the premises which characterize people and customary practices all have profound influence on the role of an administrative organization in bringing about change. Because relatively less formal attention has been paid to premises than to the other aspects of innovating organizations, in the remaining pages of this chapter I shall illustrate the theme of how basic cultural, bureaucratic, and especially professional premises bear on the problem of directed culture change. These premises, it seems to me, influence the program of the organization charged with bringing about change in at least two important ways: (1) they play a major and probably determinative role in decisions about what is thought to be a "good" program, appropriate to the needs of the recipient peoples; (2) they determine the way in which a program, once accepted, is presented to the people in question.

Premises and Project Design. Colonial officers, community development workers, health personnel, and architects and city planners often seem under a compulsion to "improve" housing, a goal equated with the visual impact of new and better design. The premises underlying this compulsion are varied, having in common only that they usually reflect the planner's ideas of what is needed, rather than those of the recipient peoples. This professional ethnocentrism, coupled with frequent failure to analyze fully the possible consequences of major changes, sometimes produces unanticipated results.

Improved Housing in New Guinea. In 1956 the colonial government of former Netherlands New Guinea began developmental work among the primitive Asmat. In order to simplify administration, provide schooling, initiate agricultural improvements, and attend to health needs, the government planned permanent villages with "improved" houses. Whereas traditional houses were built of sago leaves, the new houses were of wood, solidly constructed. In addition to visual impact, a major argument for this design was that it lent itself better to DDT residual spraying for malaria control.

Although the old houses were easier to build and repair, the design and construction of the new were well within the abilities of the people, and where a missionary or teacher tactfully used his influence a good many of them were built. It was found, however, that they developed wide cracks in floors and walls, making them colder and draftier than traditional houses. After two years it was concluded that "in these circumstances the new houses offered *greater* risk of bronchial infections and pneumonias than the old-fashioned houses. The medical disadvantages of an apparently sound social economic development programme had become clear" (Van Amelsvoort 1964:83–84). The premises underlying the design were those of the planners, and they resulted in a product ill-suited to community health.

Slum Clearance in the United States. In the United States, architects and city planners perceive the slum to be dirty, crowded, and unhealthy, something which must be "cleaned up." Their usual solution is to relocate people in new, clean, hygienic dwellings, regardless of the dwellings' location or distance from work, markets, medical clinics, and other urban centers. Their professional training teaches them to design and construct the most sanitary and efficient (i.e., lowest cost) dwellings which meet the housing standards outlined in building and zoning codes. In essence, because of the premises of their profession, they see their task to be *the removal of blight*, a view that can be quite different from the slum dwellers' view of the task. The latter might see it as providing pleasant, functional, conveniently located housing (communicated by Coral Cottage).

Agricultural Extension Work in Northern Rhodesia. The agricultural planning and extension work of British personnel in the Ministry of African Agriculture, prior to the emergence of independent Zambia in 1964, beautifully illustrates how basic cultural plus professional premises determine the form of a project. The goal of ministry officers was to increase agricultural production in order to provide a cash export crop that the colony badly needed, and to settle small numbers of villagers on large farms and make them "rational" farmers. As professionals, the officers wanted farming to be carried out according to the highest technical standards, with maximum production, accomplished with the fewest possible people. Achieving these goals, obviously, would reflect favorably on their professional skills. But such goals were not consistent with the realities of the country. Since major industry to employ displaced rural peoples will not develop in Zambia for many years, the immediate result of "rational" agriculture and fewer farmers would have been widespread unemployment.

Nevertheless, since the agricultural specialists assumed there were — in Africa as in Britain — relatively few superior people who could make outstanding farmers, they devised a program whereby individuals deemed to be in this favored class would be given title to from two hundred to four hundred acres, and would receive the bulk of agricultural help and credit. The remaining 95 per cent of village farmers were to be given a scant five acres each, which they would farm on a subsistence basis with very little advice and help from extension workers. Little thought was given to how these people would react to such discrimination, nor to what they would do with their extra time. It was assumed that this was not an agricultural problem. One can see in the planners' minds the image of the sturdy British yeoman, a type to be recreated in Central Africa to give political stability to the country.

If this plan had not been abandoned with independence, it might have increased agricultural production and lowered the number of hands needed to produce the country's food and fibre necessities. It also, in all likelihood, would have produced a revolution. To take village peoples with an egalitarian view of life and with equal land rights, and to give control of the best land to an arbitrarily chosen few, thus depriving others of a large part of their livelihood, seems sheer madness. Yet the plan was proposed, and initial steps were taken, to build a nation on this pattern. The professional goal of "rational" farming, coupled with the assumptions of the experts about human ability, produced as ill-founded a technical plan as can be imagined.

Premises and Project Presentation. The same cultural and professional assumptions that play a major role in the determination
of what constitutes "good" planning are instrumental in determining how a plan, a suggested new practice, or a project is presented
to the members of a target group. Perception lies at the heart of the
problem: planners and change agents tend to assume that a single
pattern of cognition is universal, and that recipient peoples will
interpret verbal and visual presentations according to the logic of
the agents who prepare and deliver these messages. But although
perception and cognition are universal psychological processes,
the patterns in which they operate are rooted in culture; thus
interpretations of stimuli may vary widely, both from one culture
to another and within subcultures found in complex societies, as
the following illustrations show.

Table Candles and Gracious Living. In England, before it was
customary to pre-test advertising copy, a company wished to con-
vey the idea that a food product was used not only by working class
people but also by the upper classes. In an advertising campaign
this product was shown on a dining room table lighted only by
candles, presumably a symbol of middle and upper class gracious
living. "This was not the interpretation put on the candles by many
people in the North-west of England. The advertisement was
hurriedly withdrawn after it became clear that the relatively poor
families whom it was hoped to influence interpreted the presence
of candles as a sign that the supply of illuminating gas had been
cut off for non-payment of the bill — a relatively familiar experience in this region" (Wilson 1960:6–7).

Corn Meal in West Germany. After the cessation of hostilities in
World War II, a serious food shortage prevailed in West Germany.
But when in 1946 CARE sent large shipments of food that included corn meal, the recipients, far from being grateful, were
greatly offended. "How could they dare offer us chicken feed?,"
they asked. The gift flour was perceived as an insult designed by
the victorious Americans to humiliate further a conquered nation,

for in most of Europe maize is traditionally an animal and not a human food (communicated by Ingrid Brabender).

Prenatal Care in Mexican Health Centers. The preceding two illustrations show how differing perceptions may inhibit the introduction of new ways. In this and the following illustration, we see just the opposite: how an awareness of differential perception and cognition, and of the premises that underlie behavior, often makes it possible for planners to present programs in such a way that they are likely to achieve success. In Mexico City the Ministry of Health has an important prenatal program. One major goal is to persuade women to come to health centers at the first sign of pregnancy and to return at regular intervals until delivery. Hospital rather than home delivery is a second major goal of the program. The *Maternidad Isidro Espinosa de los Reyes* is the most prestigious government hospital because of its location in the elegant Lomas de Chapultepec section of the city. Women who come to health centers early in pregnancy, and who faithfully keep all appointments, receive a card entitling them to admittance to this hospital for delivery. Women less regular in attendance, or who begin prenatal control late in pregnancy, are admitted to other hospitals, technically just as good, but in less prestigious neighborhoods. Héctor García Manzanedo, making a study of factors influencing women to utilize government maternity services, found that many mothers rigorously adhered to the rules of the health centers, not because they fully appreciated the importance of regular prenatal care but because to have their babies born in the Lomas de Chapultepec gave them great prestige. An understanding of the cognitive and perceptive patterns of these mothers, and of their value systems, made it possible to present a health program in such fashion as to increase utilization over that which would occur if a more routine take-it-or-leave-it attitude had prevailed (communicated by Dr. García).

Environmental Hygiene in Tehuantepec. In the mid-1950's the Mexican Ministry of Health, as a part of a nation-wide rural health campaign, offered to pay home owners in Tehuantepec, Oaxaca, half of the cost of installing outdoor sanitary latrines, and cement floors in their houses. The health appeal fell on deaf ears, however, and at first there was scant response to the Ministry's offer. But when the anthropologists Isabel Kelly and Héctor García Manzanedo studied the reasons for resistance to these and other proposed new health facilities in Tehuantepec, they were struck with the people's strong commercial sense and with their preoccupation with increasing their capital. The anthropologists suggested that the Ministry's emphasis be shifted from health as such to the argument that, at relatively low cost, the value of property would be significantly increased. This appealed to the business minded Tehuanos, and the latrine-cement floor program turned out to be quite successful. As with the prenatal program, an understanding of the psychological characteristics of the target group and of its social and economic values made possible achievement of program goals (communicated by Dr. García).

CONCLUSIONS

The study of bureaucracy must be added to the anthropologist's traditional object of analysis, the tribe or small community, if he is to do the best applied work. When an innovating organization is looked at as a society with its own culture, marked by formal structure, division of responsibilities, values, and unquestioned premises, it quickly becomes apparent that the form taken by a particular administrative structure will have a great deal to do with success or failure in its efforts to accomplish change. When the national, bureaucratic, and professional assumptions that underlie planning and operations, all of which tend to be taken for granted, are laid bare, they can be examined to see to what extent they actually apply to contemporary conditions. Those forms that are functional can be preserved; those that no longer play a role can be discarded, their place taken by new ways and attitudes more responsive to current needs. An understanding of the structure and functioning of bureaucracy will make it possible to avoid many of the past errors made in directed change programs.

CHAPTER 6   the interaction setting

CHANGE AGENTS AND RECIPIENT PEOPLES

For directed change to come about there must be contact between members of the innovating organization and the people toward whom a program is directed. In advertising, "contact" may be impersonal and indirect, via radio, television, and the printed word. But in the settings in which anthropologists work, almost always there is direct interaction, with change agents and recipient peoples meeting at the same time in the same place. The technical specialist normally seeks personal confrontation with the people he hopes to influence. By means of talks, by means of demonstrations and appeals to logic, he attempts to attract their attention and to make them see how his goals can be helpful to them. He tries to motivate them to desire change in the direction specified by the particular project with which he is associated, and to encourage them to work actively in achieving this change.

The personality of the technical specialist, his role as he perceives it, the accomplishments he sees as personal achievement and evidence of competence, his ability to fashion a program that may meet local needs, and his skill in presenting his program so that it seems advantageous to recipient peoples — all these elements are critical to success. For many technical specialists (as for most anthropologists), the personal contact and friendship with the people with whom they work is one of the most gratifying aspects of directed culture change assignments. These are the change agents who are most flexible in their approaches and most successful in achieving their goals.

Other change agents find personal contact with the people toward whom they direct their efforts to be a threatening and distressing experience. Technical experts who are uneasy in the presence of the people they wish to help often interpret failure to accept their recommendations as rejection of their proffered friendship, and they may fear — for good reason — that their inability to influence behavior will reflect on their professional competence. These people, however well qualified technically, usually are much less successful in developmental work than are those who can establish solid friendships marked by mutual respect with the people who are receiving aid. Obviously, the personality of the technical specialist, and the way he plays out his role when in the field with the people he hopes to influence, are enormously important in the success or failure of a program of change. One of the reasons an applied anthropologist wants to be in the field when a program is actively in progress is to be able to observe the role perception and role performance of these key people.

The anthropologist, however, does not compartmentalize his research, first making a study of the target group, then returning to the city to analyze the innovating organization, and finally coming back to the interaction setting along with the technical specialists who are now prepared for action. Ideally, at least, research swings back and forth from field to office, and, wherever he is, the anthropologist is gathering data that pertain to all three research foci. In the interaction setting, he continues to learn about the values of an innovating organization through the behavior of its technical specialists under the pressure of their field experience. Here he also learns new things about the social structure, the values, and the premises of the target group, important points that escaped him in his preliminary analyses. The prod of active intervention in a society reveals relationships, dependencies, sensitive points, and unresolved conflicts not immediately apparent when the society is in a quiescent state. It is in the interaction setting that the anthropologist has an opportunity to see how his previous hypotheses and his predictions will work out. This is, in the language of the bullring, "the moment of truth," where the interaction of technical experts and local people permits the anthropologist to judge himself and his competence in prediction.

In orienting research in the interaction setting, where the technical specialist is actively carrying out his program, I have found it helpful to visualize the major areas requiring anthropological attention as (1) the basic processes of change occurring in most rural and village areas, and in lower socioeconomic urban groups in developing countries as well; (2) the cultural, social, and psychological barriers to change, and the stimulants which overcome these barriers; (3) the social and psychological characteristics of the technical specialist, as revealed in the field, and the ways in which these characteristics affect a given program. Since the first two areas have been explored at length elsewhere (Foster 1962), here I will simply summarize some of the main conclusions, concentrating on the third topic, the behavior of the technical specialist.

THE PROCESSES OF CULTURE CHANGE

The kinds of change with which we are concerned are those generally described as due to "acculturation," that is, those which result when two or more different groups come into significant degrees of contact productive of changes in all. Planned culture change can be thought of as acculturation under forced draft, since because of project goals and deadlines, and because the very purpose of such work is to accelerate the achievement of change, the processes engendered by contact are significantly speeded up.

In non-totalitarian countries directed change programs ideally conform to democratic processes which expose people to new ways, perhaps allow them a role in planning change, and then permit them to make the personal decisions to change or not to change, with a minimum of coercion or persuasion. One reason so many directed change programs are slow in producing results is that they follow this philosophy. Change through democratic processes usually comes about more slowly than change through fiat.

At the same time we must recognize that the meeting of two systems (the innovating organization and the target group) in planned culture change situations often is not entirely equal. Former colonial administrations, for example, had very great powers of control over native peoples. Even in the more common situation of inducing change in customary habits, government bureaus have definite powers and authority (a health ministry can forcibly vaccinate), and, by virtue of official status and technical training, change agents usually have a prestige and authority not matched by local people. Usually it is an innovating organization, such as a health department, a social welfare agency, or an agricultural extension service, that defines a problem, plans a project to attack the problem, initiates contact with the people concerned, sets goals and deadlines, and uses all its resources, skill, and ingenuity in meeting these goals, whatever the degree of opposition encountered. Consultation and planning with the people whose lives are to be affected often exists less in fact than in theory.

Cross-cultural analyses of culture change situations have revealed a series of regularities that seem to occur, time after time, at different historical periods, and in settings far removed from one another; it can reasonably be assumed therefore that these regularities represent generic processes rather than a result of diffusion, and that in those situations where significant conditions are similar, similar processes will occur. The following are illustrative of these processes:

1. Cities, where the upper classes usually reside, are the principal focal points of change, and through the motivation of imitation and the desire for prestige, city and elite ways filter down to the lower classes and out to the countryside.

2. Major changes in the economic basis of livelihood, and espe-

cially the shift from subsistence to wage labor (often accompanied by migration to cities), bring about significant changes in family organization. Normally the nuclear family gains in importance and the extended family loses. Traditional responsibilities and expectations of help, widely spread through kinship and friendship networks, are reduced to a much smaller group.

3. The introduction of cash crops, with greater emphasis on market disposition of production, tends to destroy traditional cooperative work patterns based on exchanges of labor.

4. Dietary deterioration usually occurs following a shift from a subsistence to a monetary economy. In effect, the conventional food wisdom of people, developed on a trial and error basis over generations, does not serve in situations in which people buy rather than grow the bulk of their food. They must learn how to buy wisely in order to have a balanced diet.

5. Rapid change frequently promotes divisive tendencies in traditional groups, thus making cooperative efforts even more difficult than under preexisting conditions. People exposed to few outside influences and new ideas are faced with few choices about what to do as a group, and hence the opportunities for disagreement are limited. Tradition determines the paths to be followed. Faced with many new choices, as are today's villagers, the opportunities for differing judgments are vastly increased, with resulting conflicts in opinions.

BARRIERS AND STIMULANTS TO CHANGE

All societies, all communities, are constantly in tension, hosts to two kinds of forces. On the one hand are the forces that seek to maintain the status quo, to preserve the system's equilibrium, to keep it functioning with a minimum of change. On the other hand are the forces for change that prod the system into modifying and rearranging its internal structure, causing a perpetual restlessness which results in an advance from one state of equilibrium to another. In the long run, change forces always prove to be stronger, since no society remains absolutely static. But change usually does not come quickly or easily or without cost.

A basic role of the applied anthropologist is to analyze systems in order to identify and describe the conservative forces that promote the status quo (the barriers), and to discover the progressive forces (the stimulants) that in the form of human motivations and cultural conditions induce and permit people to modify their traditional behavior. When these forces in both the innovating organization and the recipient society are known, intelligent planning and successful operations are more easily achieved.

In discussing barriers to change, I have found it helpful to group them in cultural, social, and psychological categories. Important cultural barriers include the weight of tradition itself and the accompanying fatalism so often noted, an ethnocentric belief (just as prevalent among primitive peoples and peasants as among Americans) in the superiority of one's traditional ways, ideas about norms of modesty, and attitudes about pride, dignity, and face. Habitual body postures and motor patterns also frequently influence receptivity to some kinds of change.

Social barriers to change lie in the traditional obligations and expectations, based on reciprocity patterns within family, fictive kin, and friendship groups, of most preindustrial societies. According to this view of reciprocity, those who have (at the moment) share with those who (at the moment) do not. In societies where access to resources is essentially equal, it is assumed that over time everyone will contribute and receive roughly the same amount. Hence the system functions as a social security device, tiding people over bad periods at the cost of requiring them to help others when they are able to do so. But in a rapidly changing world, more able or more aggressive or more progressive people begin to acquire permanent advantages over others. If they feel constrained to continue to honor their traditional obligations, the advantages they have achieved are drained away, since their well-being is an open invitation for less fortunate or less able relatives and friends to attach themselves on a more or less permanent basis. We have seen how many potential innovators are reluctant to make economic progress because they do not wish to sever ties with their families and friends (as in the case of Filipino farmers described on page 12). Real progress for innovative people can come only when they pass over a critical psychological threshold which permits them to ignore public opinion, to fail to carry out traditional obligations, and to enjoy the fruits of their energy and ability.

Psychological barriers are especially rooted in the differences between the perceptual processes of the members of innovating organizations and those of recipient groups. Members of lower socioeconomic groups in complex societies, and primitive peoples and peasants, often interpret the probable consequences of innovation in ways quite distinct from those intended by technical experts charged with modifying prevailing practices. Government and its representatives may be perceived as threats to rather than bearers of a better life, and a gift may be interpreted as bait, a device to disarm the unwary so that he may more easily be victimized. Trained medical personnel may see a major health problem in something viewed by the people as of little importance. This is true, for example, of the Navajo Indians, a disproportionate number of whom suffer from a congenital hip defect which causes disability in later life. Yet because of cultural reasons, afflicted Navajos appear little interested in the corrective surgery that can spare them subsequent pain and suffering (McDermott, et al., 1960). Again, a change agent may execute a demonstration badly, and produce the effect opposite to that intended, since the audience perceives the actual and not the intended outcome.

Stimulants promoting change include both the individual motivations that lead people to experiment with novelty, and the creation of the basic conditions that permit change to come about in orderly fashion. Two related forces — the desire for economic gain and the desire for greater prestige — seem to be especially powerful motivations for behavior changes. A third important motivation arises from the demands of friendship. Many people try new ways simply because they have become friends with the change agent and wish to please him by doing what he asks. He has helped them, or they suspect he has the power to help them;

hence they feel it is wise and fair to do something in return. Much induced change has had nothing whatsoever to do with real conviction on the part of client group members as to its desirability; it is simply a tribute to the personal qualities of the technical expert, or a recognition of the tangible benefits he has brought to the people involved.

The creation of basic conditions permitting change refers, first, to designing programs that "fit" the local picture, that do no unnecessary violence to preexisting forms, and that can be executed without major social and cultural dislocations. Favorable basic conditions also mean such things as presenting innovations at propitious times — say, following a successful harvest when people have sufficient surplus to feel they can gamble a little on an untested but tempting novelty.

THE CHANGE AGENT AND HIS EGO GRATIFICATION

Directed change programs are carried out by technical specialists of many types. These specialists are social and cultural creatures, products of their national cultures, of their professional subcultures, and of their experiences as members of innovating organizations. They are bearers of the premises of these three systems, premises that will be instrumental in determining their definition of their roles, of the tasks incumbent to these roles, and of their role performance. Each technical expert is also a psychological entity who shares many character traits with his professional colleagues and fellow countrymen, but who in the final analysis is a unique being with psychic needs not exactly duplicated in any other person. The way in which these needs are expressed in his behavior will have a great deal to do with his effectiveness as a change agent.

A competent technical specialist, like any other professional, is proud of the contributions his field can make to human well-being, and he feels strongly that it is highly important in his society. Moreover, he takes pride in his ability to practice his profession and to perform well as a representative of his field. The

ego gratification which comes from the recognition that one is
doing well is an important element in good role performance. A
person is pleased when he feels his superiors, his professional
peers, and society at large recognize that he is doing a good job.
This desire for ego gratification is in part, of course, a practical
matter. In a bureaucracy, whether a university department of anthropology or a county public health department, promotion,
greater responsibility, and higher salaries all depend on formal recognition by others — by those with the power to confer these rewards — of the fact that a person merits promotion.

For university professors, public health personnel, and similarly
placed professionals, higher salaries have a great deal to do with
living standards. But, even for people in these middle income
brackets, promotion, increased authority, and rising salaries are
very important in another way: they are visible forms of evidence
that testify to recognition of ability. They are *symbols* of talent
and competence. In big business, highly paid executives usually
do not *need* more and more income in order to live with the com-
forts and conveniences they desire. But they are vitally concerned
with increasing their salaries because they know that, in the
corporate system in which they compete, published salaries are a
major item of comparison by which managerial talent and imagi-
nation are evaluated. A salary that goes up each year is, therefore,
the best possible assurance to the recipient that he is indeed able,
and that his ability is recognized by his organization and made
public in the business world.

Among university professors and technical specialists, salaries
are perhaps less meaningful as symbols of merit and competence,
although in the academic world at least they are becoming more
and more important. But there are other much sought after symbols, more important in university life, that serve a similar function: the size of research grants, the demand for one's services
as a consultant, the national and international meetings to which
one's way is paid, and the like.

Change agents, then, like other professionals, are very much
aware of the symbols that in their fields point to competence, and

they are concerned with recognition of good role performance. *But what is good role performance?* It is not something that exists within an individual, without reference to others; it is something that can be measured *only in relation to other people*. That is, the response of others is a basic part — probably the critical one — in assessing performance. A good professional performance means that clients respond well and that they do the kinds of things they are expected to do as a consequence of the change agent's efforts. If members of the client group do not respond as expected, the evidence suggests a poor professional performance.

Client peoples, then, have enormous powers over the professionals who work with them, even though usually they don't appreciate this fact. They have the power to *grant* or to *withhold* the evidence of ability which is so important to the professional. He, in most instances, also does not fully appreciate this psychological element in his relationship to members of the client group, although subconsciously at least he senses it. An analogy with teachers and students will perhaps clarify this point. All teachers from time to time are annoyed with, or disappointed by, their students. Examination papers are less good than expected, or term papers do not measure up to original high hopes. Teachers may feel that their students have "let them down," or have failed to appreciate the hard work that has gone into lecture preparations. Obviously, of course, students vary among themselves, as do their performances from one week to another. But the real problem is that, subconsciously at least, the teacher is upset because he knows that poor student response may well be a criticism of his ability, an indication that he hasn't done as well as he would like to have done.

So, for most professionals, the reaction of the members of the client group is enormously important; it is viewed in an emotion-free, detached way only with difficulty. Whether he likes it or not, recognizes it or not, the professional is intimately tied to the members of the group with whom he works — a peasant village or a university class — and his psychological well-being and perhaps his material comfort also will depend on how the roles implicit in this tie are played out. Unfortunately, people who occupy a higher status (in terms of these role relationships) often are reluctant to acknowledge that their performance is conditioned *by their own feelings and concern about themselves.* It is much more comforting for them to think that they struggle in their jobs, having at heart only the interests of the people among whom they work. They see themselves as selfless in their efforts, giving their all without thought to personal reward, simply because society expects them, as a duty, to do a sound job.

When clients, whether students or peasant villagers, fail to respond in the way teachers or technical specialists feel they should, the professionals tell themselves that their annoyance and disappointment are due to the fact that the interests of the client group members are jeopardized. Their anger is, in fact, due largely to a sense of personal failure, but it is diverted toward others, since almost all people are reluctant to admit that they have not done as well as they would have wished. The student or villager may or may not be jeopardizing his own best interests, but by failing to perform as the situation seems to dictate, he is certainly threatening the interests of the teacher or change agent.

An Example from High School Teaching. The psychological aspects of the professional-client relationships as represented in a high school have recently been described by Steubing. The high school teacher, Steubing says, feels he fulfills a highly important function in American society, but that he is grossly underpaid for his efforts. His principal satisfactions, therefore, come not from salary but from the recognition of his ability by fellow teachers, students, supervisors, and to a lesser extent parents. Since the performance of students is the most important measure of ability, the teacher wants as many "good" and as few "bad" students as possible. The former conform to the rules, do good work, produce what the teacher expects of them; the latter, of course, are just the opposite. Since a student's high marks are the best evidence of a teacher's ability and skill, "getting students through examinations" becomes a major teaching goal, at the expense of imparting knowledge and enthusiasm. The teacher deludes himself into thinking his concern is with scholarship; actually he is interested in his own ego gratification.

Since "good" students are a limited commodity, there is competition among teachers for them and for their time. Teachers therefore resent activities that reduce the time a student can spend on the subjects they teach. Rehearsal for a dramatic club play or a glee club concert will significantly reduce the amount of homework a student can do, often resulting in lower grades for an academic period. These lower grades, the teacher feels, are unfortunate for the student. But in addition he senses that they may be interpreted by others as reflecting on his teaching ability, even though obviously he is not to blame for the reduced study time that has contributed to the poor grades.

Teachers of "soft" subjects (such as music, drama, art, and home economics), and electives not required for college admission, resent the fact that when the chips are down students neglect these subjects in order to complete assignments in subjects critical for their future education. Since art, music, and drama are the subjects usually most visible to the public, the stakes for a good high school teacher are enormously high and, conversely, the opportunity for failure is great. When teachers in these subjects are told by a student that an extra laboratory report made it impossible for him to complete an assignment or to practice for a public concert, they feel deflated since, in effect, the student means that he feels their subjects are less important than the other. In the American high school, as Steubing describes it, we see a nearly perfect analogy to the interpersonal psychological factors that characterize the work of a professional change agent in a developmental program (Steubing 1968).

DIRECT AND INDIRECT PROFESSIONAL-CLIENT RELATIONSHIPS

People work in at least two types of settings, or professional environments, each of which produces different types of satisfactions and gratifications, and different symbols which measure and evaluate role performance. The first is a *direct* relationship between the professional and members of the client group, the ultimate consumers of his services. The second is an *indirect* relationship between the professional and the ultimate consumer. Representative of the former are physicians, nurses, health educators, teachers, agricultural extension agents, lawyers, and ministers; representative of the latter are engineers, highway designers, and architects and city planners.

Direct Relationships. Professionals whose work brings them into direct, face-to-face contact with the people toward whom their efforts are directed often find the experience richly rewarding. When evidence of client satisfaction and appreciation are immediately forthcoming, the professional knows he is doing his work well, for the act itself provides the feedback which shows beyond doubt how he is doing. But if acceptance is more personal, rejection is more obvious. A teacher who fails to attract good students, a physician who can't hold his patients, or an agricultural extension agent who is ignored by farmers knows from day to day how he is doing. If he is perceptive, he sees the need to improve his methods, to try better ways to reach his professional goals.

Not all professionals whose work calls for a direct relationship with clients are able to achieve the effective contacts they may desire. Other avenues, however, are open to them. A university professor who senses he is doing poorly in teaching may persuade himself that research is the really important thing, and he may retreat as much as possible into this activity to avoid the distress that accompanies poor class reaction. Medical doctors may also turn to research, or to X rays, laboratory work, or anesthesiology for the same reason, that by so doing they can avoid what has become a distressing situation.

Indirect Relationships. Unlike those professionals who have direct contact with the members of the client group, with the ultimate consumers of services, professionals like city planners, highway designers, and engineers deal with intermediaries such as city commissions, citizens' committees, and school boards. Their immediate "client" is a go-between who separates them from the ultimate consumer of their services — the public. These professionals, while spared the pain of immediately realizing that they have performed poorly, are also denied the satisfactions that come from direct contact with the people toward whom their efforts are directed. Ultimately their professional satisfactions may come in part from a grateful if amorphous public, but more often they appear to come from other sources — from the elegance of designs, from the acceptance of designs by commissions capable of having them transformed into structures, from the reproduction of plans or photographs of finished works in professional journals and the public press. Possibly peer approval is the greatest source of ego gratification for this type of professional. If so, that helps explain the frequent criticism directed toward planners and designers: they consider people only as statistics, to be manipulated like all other factors in the situation.

The symbolic importance of design as an indicator of professional ability may also explain the excess of overplanning sometimes seen in international development (e.g., Foster 1962:181). Without boards of supervisors, citizens' committees, and the other customary checks of American life, a planner in an overseas setting sometimes sees his opportunity not as one in which he can meet the needs of the local people, but rather as one in which he can achieve the design of a lifetime, in which he can execute the really "perfect" plan. Needless to say, plans like these usually are ill-adapted to local needs.

SUMMARY

The interaction setting affords a highly productive research focus for an applied anthropologist. Here he can study the processes of change under forced circumstances, so that sequences that normally take months or years can be compressed into much shorter periods. With previous study of the premises and mode of operations of the innovating organization, and with knowledge of the people being aided, he can test his hypotheses about change in this near-laboratory setting. Good hypotheses will be confirmed by what actually happens in the interaction setting. Less good hypotheses will need to be modified or perhaps discarded.

Particularly important to the anthropologist is his opportunity to study the behavior of the change agent, as a tripartite product of national, professional, and bureaucratic cultures, and as a psychic individual with intense ego-gratification needs. The ways in which the members of the recipient group grant or withhold the evidences of the change agent's competence, and of his reaction under stressful conditions, afford rich opportunities to add to knowledge about human behavior. Finally, the sensitive applied anthropologist will recognize that he too, like the change agent, is much concerned with his performance, and that symbols of approval or disapproval, acceptance or rejection, both by members of the recipient group and of the innovating organization, will have much to do with his psychological well-being and his ability to function effectively.

CHAPTER 7

CHAPTER 7   applied anthropology
            and professional status

THE STATUS OF APPLIED ANTHROPOLOGY

"The acceptance of a social role may be facilitated or retarded by the degree of status ascribed to it" (Young 1964:229). The relatively low status accorded by many anthropologists to applied anthropological work has slowed the development of this branch of the discipline. Applied research is viewed by a majority of anthropologists as less profound, less scientifically vital, and hence less worthy of applause than research seen as having no immediate practical ends. This attitude has inhibited the development of applied anthropology teaching and research in universities, and it has discouraged interest in the field among budding anthropologists.

Scant formal attention is paid in American universities to applied anthropology, its character, its methods, and its contributions to society and science. Even in large departments, applied anthropology offerings normally are limited to an undergraduate course or two and perhaps an occasional graduate seminar. When students, frequently from other disciplines, ask about the specialized training that would help fit them for international and developmental work, they are told that they must take a full anthropology program, and that they can pick up a bit of application along the way.

Only in time of war has it been fully respectable for anthropologists to devote themselves wholeheartedly to nontheoretical goal-oriented research. Only rarely does an anthropologist like to be known primarily for his applied rather than his theoretical research. More often than not, it is a reputation firmly established from theoretical research that permits an anthropologist to speak with authority on applied problems. In other words, after an anthropologist has "made good" in conventional research, he can enjoy the luxury of applied research without fearing for his reputation. In such fields as public health, medicine, education, agricultural extension, social welfare, and community development, the utility of anthropology (and the other behavioral sciences) is increasingly recognized, and calls are made for the services of anthropologists. Yet to many anthropologists, such applied work lacks scientific respectability. An anthropologist, they argue, should stick to his last of theoretical investigation, leaving utilization of his discoveries to administrators and technical specialists in the fields concerned. A few investigators even seem to delight in the feeling that their research has no apparent utility.

This is unfortunate, for it is apparent that sociocultural and psychological data — the stuff of applied anthropology — can, like all other bodies of organized data, appeal to scientifically oriented people in two rather different ways. For one group the extant data and theory of a given field are simply the jumping-off point for the gathering of more data and the elaboration of better and more comprehensive theory; that is, the scientific pursuit is an end in itself. The quest for knowledge drive of the theoretical scientist is laudable, and it is likely that his society sooner or later will make practical use of all he discovers. In fact, a complex society which did not make practical use of the findings of pure science could not long exist, nor could it continue to support pure scientific research. It is precisely the ability of a social system to utilize scientific knowledge constructively that makes possible widespread support of theoretical research, not to mention rising standards of living and improvements in human well-being.

For the second group of scientifically oriented people, science is a means to an end as well as an end in itself. The beauty of data and theory, and their challenge, lie in the ways in which they can be turned to the improvement of man's state. They involve value judgments of a practical nature. To illustrate, many scientifically trained and scientifically oriented people, such as epidemiologists, physicians, educators, and a few anthropologists and sociologists, believe that it is desirable for a health educator to try to change the health beliefs and practices of Indian villagers, and that it is scientifically challenging to use data and theory about human behavior, as well as research methods from the behavioral sciences, in order to achieve this goal. This practical drive toward knowledge for man's betterment, like the quest for knowledge drive, is laudable and should not be discouraged for reasons of status and false pride. Society needs both types of researchers, and the individual who freely selects his field according to temperament and interests, uninhibited by professional pressures stemming from the prestige and status attached to a role, will certainly make the greatest contributions of which he is capable and hence best serve his society.

It is possible that there are able, well-trained anthropologists, in control of the data and theory of the field, who are not particularly original in theory building, but who, imbued with the status valuation of the field, cling to what they imagine to be the greater scientific respectability of the "pure" side of the science. If anthropologists were less status conscious, some of these people would be in goal-oriented programs where they might be happier and where their scientific contributions might be more substantial. The converse is doubtless also true, although to a lesser extent. There are certainly anthropologists whose careers have been largely of an applied nature who, if chance had dropped them into the intensely competitive milieu of a great university, would have made outstanding theoretical contributions of a type their applied careers did not encourage.

SOME REASONS FOR LOW STATUS

With these thoughts in mind, let us consider the factors that have conspired to relegate applied anthropological work to a rather low level. Then we will show that this status valuation is unjustified and harmful to the best interest of the field at large, including theory building. The applied scientist justifies himself and his role in society in a way that the layman understands with little difficulty: he is using science to raise standards of living and to contribute to human happiness and well-being, however difficult these words may be to define. The theoretical scientist, on the other hand, justifies himself and his role in society, and his right to be supported by that society, in a way that is often difficult for the layman to comprehend. This justification rests on a philosophical and unverifiable judgment: the pursuit of knowledge for its own sake is a morally acceptable end, indeed the highest value in science. Absolute truth, insofar as it can be recognized and established, and regardless of its consequences for society, must be the scientist's supreme goal. Truth is achieved through research in which previously unknown facts are discovered and existing knowledge is ordered in new and meaningful patterns and relationships. This research is "value-free," and only complete and impartial objectivity, untainted by work-a-day considerations, will produce valid results.

This view of science and the role of the scientist is, of course, a value judgment in itself. As Young says, "Scientists have developed a tendency to accept uncritically the dictum that what is good for science is good for humanity. This may be true, but it is no more than an assumption based on personal interpretation of relatively recent human history" (*ibid.*, 231). Some years ago a president of General Motors outraged the country with the statement, made in all sincerity, that "what is good for General Motors is good for the nation." In a general way he undoubtedly was right, just as in a general way the theoretical scientist is right. Almost everyone is convinced that his own values, views, mode of operation, customary behavior, and rights and privileges are basi-

cally supportive of the society in which he lives. This implicit assumption is questioned only under the most unusual circumstances. Scientists are no exception: it is comforting to them to
know that what they do, and what they like to do, is of great
value to their nation.

Unfortunately, once a scientist accepts this attitude uncritically,
as he usually does by the time he finishes his training, he may
feel smug with regard to the activities of lesser mortals, and wish
more and more to disassociate himself from contemporary social
and economic problems. C. P. Snow has said, "Pure scientists have
by and large been dimwitted about engineers and applied science. They couldn't get interested. They wouldn't recognize that
many of the problems were as intellectually exacting as pure
problems, and that many of the solutions were as satisfying and
beautiful. Their instinct — perhaps sharpened in this country
[England] by the passion to find a new snobbism wherever possible, and to invent one if it doesn't exist — was to take it for
granted that applied science was an occupation for second-rate
minds. I say this more sharply because thirty years ago I took precisely that line myself. The climate of thought of young research
workers in Cambridge then was not to our credit. *We prided ourselves that the science we were doing could not, in any conceivable circumstances, have any practical use. The more firmly one
could make that claim, the more superior one felt*" (Snow 1963:
35–36 — emphasis added).

Few if any anthropologists go so far as to pride themselves on
their work's total lack of practical utility, but a strong current of
thought has long held, and to some extent continues to hold, that
to the extent the anthropologist steps out of his "pure" science
role he compromises his scientific respectability and claim to the
support of his society. E. E. Evans-Pritchard, a leading British social anthropologist, has voiced this opinion: "It may be held that
it is laudable for an anthropologist to investigate practical problems. Possibly it is, but if he does so he must realize that he is no
longer acting within the anthropological field but in the non-
scientific field of administration. Of one thing I feel quite certain:

that no one can devote himself wholeheartedly to both interests; and I doubt whether anyone can investigate fundamental and practical problems at the same time" (Evans-Pritchard 1946:93).

The late M. J. Herskovits shared this point of view. In reviewing *Man's Most Dangerous Myth*, in which Ashley Montagu seeks a solution for the American race problem, he wrote that Montagu should "be content to remain the anthropologist, and not aspire to follow the dim, treacherous path of what is coming to be termed the 'social engineer'" (Herskovits 1946:268). The scientist, Herskovits felt, must realize that "the search for truth must come before all else. The debt we owe the society that supports us must be made in terms of long-time payments, in our fundamental contributions toward an understanding of the nature and processes of culture and, through this, to the solution of some of our own basic problems" (Herskovits 1936:222; requoted 1948: 653).

There are several explanations for the views stated here (which illustrate those of many other anthropologists) and for the relatively low status of applied anthropology in general. Some of these explanations are found in the organizational structure and premises of anthropology itself, while others stem from wider considerations. We will discuss four possible explanations: values and ethics, individual freedom, prestige levels in science, and relationships between pure and applied research.

Values and Ethics. Anthropologists are trained in a scientific environment in which cultural relativity is a basic premise. They therefore are reluctant to pass judgment on the relative merits of the ways of life of other people. Yet the rationale for directed culture change programs is that technical experts can and should evaluate the practices of other people and decide which ones should be modified. Many anthropologists find the "hands off" versus "meddling in the lives of others" dilemma difficult to resolve. In the past at least, scientific values have seemed to constitute less of a problem than cultural values, and a reluctance to grapple with the latter unquestionably has placed a brake on applied work. (Ethical questions are further explored in the following chapter.)

Individual Freedom. Anthropology professors experience a minimum of supervision in their professional lives and a maximum of freedom in determining the use of their time, the research they will do, and the uses to which this research will be put. They find a time-clock setting confining and perhaps degrading. Yet in doing applied work they may be asked to keep regular office hours, to acknowledge an unaccustomed degree of supervision, and to conform to the administrative norms of the organization that has hired them. In the bureaucratic world degrees of authority and supervision exercised and accepted tell us a great deal about the status levels of organizational roles. Perhaps the degree of supervision anthropologists experience in some applied settings symbolizes to them a lesser status than they enjoy in the relative freedom of a university.

Prestige Levels Within Science. Regardless of precise wording, scholars agree about what science is. Conant has described it broadly as "a series of interconnected conceptual schemes which arose originally from experimentation or careful observation and were fruitful of new experiments or observations" (Conant 1948: 78). Because of his inclusion of "careful observation" as well as experimentation as a valid aspect of methodology, Conant's definition is particularly important to anthropology. The philosopher James Feibleman defines science more precisely as "that division of culture which conducts the search among facts, through the method of hypothesis, experiment and verification, for tendencies, laws and causes, leading to the prediction of events and the control over phenomena and, at advanced stages of development, involving mathematically-formulated theories to account for instrumentally-discovered data" (Feibleman 1948:38). This definition more nearly corresponds to the layman's image of scientific research, involving, as it does, laboratories, experiments, quantitative data, and mathematical expression of results. This is the way in which most research in the natural sciences, and some in the social sciences, is carried out.

But by no means all phenomena are amenable to investigation by controlled experiments in laboratories. In anthropology, and in other fields as diverse as geology and astronomy, Conant's "careful observation" has been the principal source of information. The method of so-called "participant observation," in which the anthropologist immerses himself in the life of a community and uses all his senses to record and try to understand what is going on, is nothing more than "careful observation." Vastly oversimplifying, we can say therefore that there are two basic research procedures: that of laboratory experimentation, with elaborate instrumentation, and that of "natural history," the latter based on observation utilizing a minimum of instrumentation. These are not absolute categories, of course, but the difference between them is clear. Regardless of research procedures, every scientist ultimately is concerned with propositions expressing the relationships and regularities that appear in his data, stated tentatively as hypotheses and confirmed, modified, or rejected through rigorous testing which can in turn be experimental or observational. The propositions that survive are accepted as scientific laws (which are themselves always conditional and tentative, subject to modification or abandonment when new knowledge so requires).

It is apparent that disciplines based on laboratory experiment have been far more successful in stating scientific laws than those disciplines, anthropology among them, that must rely on careful observation including measurement under less controlled situations. In fact, the traditional American anthropological view, first enunciated by Boas, has been that it is extremely unlikely that social and cultural laws *ever* will be derived, except in the most general sense. This extreme position is weakening, and some anthropologists, notably Barnett, are optimistic about the possibilities of formulating sociocultural laws, at least as they apply to "processes" (Barnett 1965).

Nevertheless, the traditional view of the dichotomy between laboratory, experimental sciences that produce laws, and natural history, observational sciences that do not, has been very important in the formation of the prestige scale of science. According to this prestige scale, those disciplines which produce laws are considered to be more scientific (and hence of higher status) than those which produce only descriptive generalizations. In anthropology and other social sciences the image of the successful research physicist or his counterpart in chemistry or biology tends, consciously or unconsciously, to represent the goal toward which we feel we should strive. The precision with which experimentation is carried out in the laboratory and the fashion in which complex data are reduced to economical statements fill us with envy. We like to consider ourselves scientists, but sometimes, in the face of such dazzling performances, we wonder how good our claim really is.

It is probable that the vehemence with which some anthropologists insist upon the wide value gulf between theoretical and applied work may represent in part an attempt to achieve what we imagine to be the only form of scientific respectability. We cannot duplicate the results of men who work in laboratory based sciences, but we can align ourselves with them by insisting that their goals and values are also ours. However subconsciously, we may run the risk of seeing applied work as potentially contaminating, since modern scientists and the society in which they flourish agree that applied work is on a lower level than pure research. An outstanding theoretical physicist can hope to receive the Nobel Prize, but the imaginative and daring engineer who develops radar, or builds a bridge previously declared impossible, can aspire to no such reward. By eschewing application, the anthropologist may hope to remain just a little nearer to the angels. Unfortunately, however much he narrows the gap, the Nobel Prize will always elude him.

Relationships between Theoretical and Applied Anthropology. In Chapter 2 we sketched two models representing the relationships between theoretical and applied science in general, and anthropology in particular. The first portrayed the popular idea of direct transfer of theory and data to practical problems; the second showed how the relationship, in anthropology at least, is much more complex. We saw from the second model that, although theory certainly feeds into practice, practice also flows back along the same line, so that basic theory often is strengthened by the results of practical research. The simpler model, however, was implicit in much earlier anthropological thinking — a fact which has left its impress on contemporary thinking, even though some of the following quotations may no longer fully reflect the ideas of their authors.

"When we talk of Applied Anthropology we mean a body of knowledge that is *applicable* to the practical undertakings of administrator, missionary, educationist, settler or trader" (E. W. Smith 1934:xxxiv). "Any analysis of what has come to be known as 'applied anthropology,' therefore, primarily involves *application* of our ethnological knowledge . . ." (Herskovits 1936:216). "The applied anthropologist, in theoretical distinction from the research anthropologist, *applies* his science . . ." (Lantis 1945:20). "In any strict sense the phrase 'applied anthropology in government' must refer to the actual *application* of anthropological knowledge by those administratively responsible in the formulation and execution of government policy" (Forde 1953:841 — emphasis added in all quotations).

A corollary of this idea is that the utility of application is dependent on anthropology's preexisting theoretical achievements. Thus, "The value of an applied anthropology must depend on the extent of the exact knowledge which we have and are able to apply . . ." (Radcliffe-Brown 1931:278). ". . . it is common ground that the quality of service which social anthropology can render to colonial administrations is dependent on its theoretical achievements" (Forde 1953:861). "I would urge . . . that the anthropologist should restrict his research to the investigation of scientific problems for the reasons that the value of social anthropology to the arts of politics and administration must depend on its theoretical advance" (Evans-Pritchard 1946:93).

The "Clinical" vs. the "Engineering" Model. If, however, we reject what we imagine to be the exact sciences model, perhaps substituting for "applied" some more neutral word (such as "operational"), the picture becomes clearer. Some years ago Alexander Leighton pointed out that the relationship between theory and application, between pure and applied research, is not necessarily the same in all science, and that an apt model for one may be quite unsatisfactory for another. His views have given rise to what today in the behavioral sciences we call the "clinical" and the "engineering" models to distinguish basic patterns of relationships. Drawing upon his experience as a physician as well as an anthropologist, Leighton wrote about the importance of clinical research to medicine:

> In this field, medical practice and medical research are combined, each to the advantage of the other. It is only in the clinic that the results of the laboratory sciences have their full testing and this may involve profound changes, or complete rejection of hypotheses as well as the firm establishment of previously tentative conclusions. . . . By the compilation and analysis of many such records theory and therapeutic practice are both benefited. Most important of all, there are many instances wherein the decision as to a program can be made on a scientific basis with the result that the clinic is a place where the opportunities are exceedingly rich for direct experimentation with human beings. Some of our basic knowledge of brain function, for example, has been derived from clinical research through taking advantage by observation of accidents and through experiments in treatment. Such experiments must, of course, be responsible and give the welfare of the individual patient primary consideration, but they are nevertheless rewarding for scientific purposes (Leighton 1946:668).

Leighton goes on to suggest the theoretical-to-applied model that is increasingly accepted as the most suitable for anthropology:

> It seems to me that applied social sciences can well be the meeting place of both science and practice as in clinical research. Participation in administrative programs through planning, execution and follow-up observation often presents a unique opportunity for careful compilation of data and for a degree of experimentation

that is not possible elsewhere. It may be that under such circumstances discoveries regarding the nature of society and culture can be made in a manner similar to that noted in connection with brain function. Moreover, social theories can be reduced to working hypotheses leading to predictions that are testable by the observation of subsequent events. Through such a series of steps, science as well as the techniques of application should advance (*ibid.* :668).

The implications of Leighton's suggestion are clear: in anthropology, the relations between theory and application are not like traffic on a one-way street. The correct model is that of a wide avenue with traffic in both directions — of theory aiding the practical worker whose field situation and experiences feed back into the basic corpus of theory. This model, of course, does not apply solely to anthropology or the behavioral sciences, for there is and always has been a great deal of interaction between theory and practice in all science. Thus, Greek geometry arose from concern with land surveying problems in Egypt, where the Nile floods made conventional boundary marks largely useless. And mathematical probability theory owes much to professional gamblers who wished to know the odds in games of chance (Feibleman 1966:305).

During the years since Leighton's suggestion of a clinical rather than an engineering model to conceptualize relationships between theoretical and applied anthropology, other anthropologists and behavioral scientists have voiced similar opinions. The late S. F. Nadel, who possessed one of the keenest theoretical minds in the field, believed that "the fairly clear-cut division between two branches of science, 'pure' and 'applied,' which seems to work well in the natural sciences, is far more blurred and problematic in anthropology.... The anthropologist who turns his attention to practical issues cannot simply 'apply' methods and theories worked out by others; rather, he may face a situation which presents him with new problems of theory and method, so that he must 'do basic research at the same time'" (Nadel 1953:14). Nadel, like Leighton, saw applied work as an exciting challenge: ". . . far from retarding scientific advance, [it] may speed it up — through offering chances for testing methods and hypotheses and through drawing attention to new problems" (*ibid.*:15).

The sociologist Alvin Gouldner questions whether, in applied social science, the principles and theory of basic disciplines are in fact applied to practical problems. For, as he points out, although we have a very healthy applied social science, we have remarkably few validated laws or broad generalizations to explain its success. "There seems to be no close correlation, therefore, between the development of generalizations by the pure disciplines and the multiplication of opportunities for, and varieties of, applied sociology" (Gouldner 1956:170). He suggests, quite correctly I think, that applied work, to the extent that it is based on theory, makes use of concepts rather than of generalized propositions of pure social science. For example, in marketing research use is made of the concept of social classes, rather than of specific propositions about social class behavior, to aid in analysis of differential consumption habits.

Moreover, says Gouldner, even with a full-blown social science it is not certain that all theoretical systems or conceptual schemes would have equal relevance and value for applied work; such a science might be organized around concepts and models only partially useful in the applied field. "An applied social science is above all concerned with the prediction and production of social and cultural change" (*ibid.*:171), yet many of the contemporary models of pure sociology have little or nothing to say about this subject. "Applied social science requires concepts enabling it to deal with change, while much of pure social science today is oriented to the analysis of stable social structures in their equilibrium" (*ibid.*:171). Since theoretical social science does not provide a sufficient framework for applied studies, it follows that the social scientist working in the latter field must be prepared to build at least a part of his relevant theory from his own experiences and observations.

Gouldner suggests that an example of this is psychoanalysis, "perhaps the most successful of the applied psychologies," which did not develop through transferring established principles to clinical problems but rather has been marked from its beginning by conceptual and theoretical innovations. Freud, he points out, developed his pure theory from his practical experience as a clinician (*ibid.*:171–172). Using this analogy, Gouldner, like Leighton, concludes that a clinical rather than an engineering model is best suited to conceptualize the relationships between theory and practice in much social science.

IMPLICATIONS OF THE CLINICAL MODEL

Once we abandon the idea that applied anthropology is nothing more than a mechanistic transfer of data and theory to practical problems, exciting vistas open up. We see that working in an applied setting offers opportunities for research experience not readily achieved in more traditional settings, that it provides the stimulus of penetrating questions from professionals in other fields, that it broadens the range of themes we study, and that it drives us to improved research methods. At one level of applied work there are opportunities to test hypotheses. At another level, and through the feedback principle, new ideas and data which stimulate theory building emerge from such research. That applied investigations can be so rewarding should not be startling. All human behavior is of potential interest to the anthropologist. By convention, by tacit agreement with other social sciences, and by reason of limitations in money and manpower, anthropological research covers only a tiny segment of the arc of human behavior — traditionally, primitive and peasant peoples in small communities. From this small sample we make so bold as to speak of developing laws of human behavior. Yet the distinctive thing about anthropology is not so much its traditional objects of study as its way of looking at a functioning social system. This "way of looking at a functioning social system," although it emerged from the study of simple peoples, knows no limits. In fact, the wider the variety of systems examined, the more broadly based our theory will be.

More Varied Research Settings. In applied research, an anthropologist works where the action agency works, and he directs his attention to those spots deemed critical in planning and operations. Not infrequently this involves village analyses of the type the anthropologist knows well. But increasingly research settings consist of city or county health departments and the populations toward which they direct their efforts, of mental hospitals, of business offices, of schools. Like tribes and peasant communities, these are social systems, and it is reasonable to hypothesize that, in structure, function, and dynamic processes, the same patterns will be found in all. But we will know this only after a great deal of research in these nontraditional social systems has been carried out.

Of all these broadened research settings, none is more important than that of the innovating organization itself. This new awareness seems to have resulted almost completely from applied work. Initially anthropologists studied change largely in terms of what went on within the societies they were analyzing, viewing innovation as something which spontaneously appeared from within or which diffused in an impersonal manner from some outside source. But, in the colonial setting, anthropologists began to learn that they had to pay specific attention to the form, values, and goals of Europeans. In Africa, as Forde points out, "The anthropologists . . . became students of the colonial administration, in that they included in their field of inquiry the effects on African societies of actions initiated and sustained by European agencies and personnel, whether governmental, commercial, or missionary. They studied the views and behavior of Europeans as actors in the situation as well as those of the Africans" (Forde 1953:849).

Not only did anthropologists study colonial administrations, but in applied work they had full access to the workings of these administrations. Formal ties made it possible to be participant observers within the social system of European government in Africa. Without these ties the intimate contact with the system studied which is basic to the anthropological methodology would have been difficult if not impossible to achieve.

Independently, American anthropologists working in applied

settings also discovered the importance of knowing the donor culture, and the opportunities for studying it when one was a member of the innovating or administrative organization itself. Leighton, for example, has well described this awakening among the anthropologists who worked for the War Relocation Authority in camps east of the Sierras to which West Coast Japanese were removed early in World War II (Leighton 1945). Richard Adams was one of the first American anthropologists to show precisely how the study of the innovating organization, made possible by association with it, permitted much fuller comprehension of a complex social and human problem. His research was designed to uncover the strong resistances to a nutrition and social work program in a Guatemalan Indian village. He found that, "The important issue in this case is that, prior to investigation, the field team and other members of the organization tended to place the blame for failures on the Indians; *actually, the trouble lay within the organization of the field team itself*, and the Indians were little more than uncomfortable bystanders in the affair" (Adams 1953:11 — emphasis added). In a somewhat comparable study, Simmons shows clearly how the organization and work assignments of staff members in a public health center in Chile were important factors in determining who did and who did not take advantage of the clinic's facilities (Simmons 1955). Simmons' formal attachment to the Chilean Ministry of Health (through his employment by the United States technical aid mission in Chile) made possible the inside analysis resulting in these conclusions.

The Stimulus of Professionals in Other Fields. Of human behavior, many kinds of questions can be asked. In academic settings anthropologists ask one kind, psychologists another kind, and sociologists still another kind. Through personal contact with university colleagues, and through acquaintance with behavioral science literature, we have a good idea of the range of these questions and of their meaning to our particular interests. But this does not exhaust the possibilities. Lawyers, doctors, public health specialists, agriculturalists, and community developers all ask additional questions. It is good for the anthropologist to be able to listen to these questions. They are asked by able and intelligent people whose sense of problem is in no way inferior to that of behavioral scientists. Many of these questions, the anthropologist finds, bear on his own thinking, and they often suggest lines of research that have not yet occurred to him. Economic planners and public health specialists may ask if the level of human fertility is essentially the same in all developing countries. That is, to illustrate, do village women in India and Mexico produce the same average numbers of children during their reproductive lives? If so, lessons about development, capital investment, and health measures may be readily transferred from one country to the other. If not, if the differences are significant, what is learned in one country may be of less importance for the other. In many Mexican villages studied by anthropologists, municipal and church vital statistics records will make possible the demographic analyses that are needed. The recognition of this need may stimulate anthropologists to exploit more fully these rich data. Association with the planners, administrators, and technical experts in directed change programs inevitably sensitizes the anthropologist to new problems, new areas of data, and new research possibilities.

The Widening Range of Research Topics. The scope and subject matter of anthropology are the result of past history and current fad. In this perspective it is clear that contemporary anthropology owes much more to the stimulation of applied research than is often recognized. During the first three decades of this century anthropologists were interested in kinds of problems rather different from those which interest them today. Most of today's problems were present fifty years ago, but we had not yet recognized their importance. Shortly after the establishment of the International Institute of African Languages and Cultures (see pages 190–192) Malinowski called attention to "an anthropological No-man's land" which included primitive economics, primitive jurisprudence, questions of land tenure, and African education, all topics on which administrators badly needed information but which had been little studied by anthropologists (Malinowski 1929:23). These, and related topics, have come in subsequent years to have great importance to anthropology, as the following examples will show.

Acculturation. It is not accidental that acculturation (or "culture contact," to use the British expression) theory began to take shape shortly after anthropologists first devoted their attention to the practical problems of colonial administration. Acculturation describes the processes that occur when two (or more) previously separate societies come into contact with each other with sufficient intensity and over sufficient time to produce significant changes in either or both. It is, of course, a contact situation particularly amenable to study in colonial settings and, in the United States, among Indian tribes as they have reacted to American culture.

Most applied anthropological research involves analyzing dynamic processes of culture change. The same is true of acculturation studies, and the basic theories that emerge from the two fields are in fact identical. A potential innovation, whether spontaneous or consciously presented to the members of a society, is subject to the same processes of perception, evaluation, and incorporation or rejection. In traditional acculturation studies, anthropologists have only occasionally witnessed an innovation, from presentation to acceptance or rejection. More often they have reconstructed a series of changes, basing their reconstructions on oral tradition, written records, and similar evidence, a method that documents *what* has happened but not necessarily *how* it happened. In contrast, since in directed culture change programs usually there is pressure behind potential innovations, the processes of acceptance or rejection are speeded beyond those that normally prevail. The anthropologist interested in acculturation theory obviously is in a strategic position if association with a technical aid program permits him to observe in a short time a series of innovations that under other conditions might spread over a decade or longer.

Political Structure and Legal Forms. Forty years ago and less, the average ethnography written by an American anthropologist about American Indians contained a brief section on political structure, probably called "Chieftainship" or something of the sort. The early British anthropologists also dealt summarily with the subject. Law usually was treated in even briefer fashion. But with the extension of Indirect Rule over most of British Africa, and with growing concern in the United States about problems of Indian administration, there arose a need for a more precise understanding of the nature of tribal political structures, of communication channels, of concepts of authority, and of indigenous legal practices and theory. Our interest in these fields certainly would have developed without the impetus of the needs of colonial and Indian administrators, but it would have come less rapidly, and perhaps would have achieved less importance to contemporary social theory.

Economics. The study of a wide variety of problems in comparative economics has been furthered by the need for information by action-oriented agencies. Forde has told how in West Africa the problems of colonial governments pointed up the need for a much clearer understanding of the social systems, the customary rules of land tenure, and the economic problems of the people concerned (Forde 1953:853). The Indians Claims Cases (see pages 209–210) tried in California to show even more clearly how the demands of contemporary problems may make for better anthropology. For more than fifty years anthropologists had worked systematically to describe the aboriginal cultures of that state, and the published reports, in number and attention to minute detail, are not surpassed for any comparable area in the world. Nevertheless, when the specifics on land ownership under aboriginal conditions were argued in court, the data proved to be so deficient that a good case could be made for almost any point of view. It is certain that, had the Indians Claims Cases been fought out fifty years earlier, our knowledge of aboriginal land ownership in California would be far superior to what it is. Moreover, with this kind of stimulus, theories about law, possession, land utilization, and ecology would have developed at a much earlier date.

It also seems reasonable to assume that the problems stemming from the increase in market (as opposed to subsistence) crops in much of the newly developing world, the growth of migrant labor for fields and mines, the establishment of factories in previously nonindustrialized areas, and the consequent flood of workers to cities, have all stimulated anthropological interest in a host of topics subsumed under the general label of "urbanization." Here we have found, perhaps predictably, that the classic models of urbanization in America formulated by Louis Wirth and his colleagues and successors are only partially applicable in Africa, Asia, and Latin America. An initially applied problem has generated its own theoretical innovations.

Psychological Anthropology. Culture and personality, and "national character" studies owe much to the applied setting, and especially to the demands of a war situation in which it was deemed desirable to be able to predict, however roughly, the behavior of nationals of enemy countries. Speaking specifically of national character analyses, Margaret Mead says categorically, "They take both their form and methods from the exigencies of the post-1939 world political situation" (Mead 1953:642).

The relationships between individual character and culture are equally interesting today to a wide variety of people, including anthropologists, psychologists, economists, and national planners. The questions they ask include: Why is an entrepreneurial spirit so often lacking in traditional societies? What social, cultural, and psychological factors stimulate development of an entrepreneurial spirit? How does the cognitive orientation of a group bear upon its ability to perceive advantage in new practices in health behavior, improved farming methods, and higher education? Applied anthropological research is helping to supply answers to these questions and others like them.

Improved Research Methods. In addition to concern with new topics and problems, applied investigations have pushed us to seek better research designs and methods. In recent years anthropologists have been much more willing to learn and to use the methods of other social sciences, especially those that can be applied to large aggregates of population, such as African tribes, where traditional participant observation and long residence in a small community are not in themselves adequate to the task. To study more than a few hundred or at most a couple of thousand people requires samples, questionnaires, statistical analysis, and a team approach, none of which has been a part of the traditional anthropological methodology, but all of which have had an invigorating and constructive effect on the field.

Again, the exigencies of circumstances have taught us that with new and different definitions of problems, it is possible in many situations to obtain meaningful data and ideas in far less time than is customarily thought necessary. For example, the Smithsonian anthropologists who engaged in the public health research described in Chapter 1 found that, with a comparative team approach carrying out research in several countries, and building on a broad base of generalized anthropological knowledge about Latin America, they were able to learn much about the significant social relationships in medical settings and about the nature and quality of folk medical belief, quite apart from the specific recommendations they made to the Institute of Inter-American Affairs.

Applied work also has stimulated interest in the analysis of the social systems of action oriented bureaucracies, as we pointed out earlier in this chapter, and has produced methodological improvements. Culture and society are remarkably elusive concepts; except in the simplest human groups they are so complex that they can be explored in only the most superficial fashion. Ease of study is, of course, one reason why anthropologists traditionally work with small, usually nonliterate societies: they are real cultures, but with many of the complexities stripped away. But, for obvious reasons, the generalizations that have been made about primitive societies are only partially applicable to complex industrial societies. Occasionally bold workers such as the Lynds or Lloyd Warner will tackle a small city, but this also is only a partial research answer to our desire to understand better the forms of social articulation, the values, the goals, and the motivations that characterize contemporary American life. In the small systems of hospitals and offices we have, somewhat as among primitives, societies and cultures in miniature. These institutions are bits of national cultures, which can be studied and analyzed effectively with traditional research methods. The obvious need to study innovating bureaucracies in action programs will redound to the theoretical benefit of the social sciences, by giving us increasing numbers of analyses of such social systems.

SUMMARY

The relatively low status enjoyed by applied anthropology is based in large part on an erroneous idea of the relationships between theoretical and applied science. Applied anthropology does not represent the mechanical application of theory and data to practical situations, as is sometimes thought to be the case. It represents an instance of a "clinical" model of relationship, in which practice affords opportunity for testing theory, and in which data gathered in a "clinical" setting feed back into the corpus of basic theory. The demands of applied anthropological work have resulted in better research methods and in the extension of fields of interest to areas of culture previously little studied. As a result of the stimulus of applied research, anthropological data and theory are far more varied and far richer than would otherwise be the case. Future applied research will result in even greater contributions to the field at large.

CHAPTER 8   problems of cooperation
in action research

DISCIPLINES AND PROFESSIONS

"No matter how tactfully it is phrased, the truth is that anthropologists and administrators do not, on the whole, get along well together" (Barnett 1956:49). Although in my experience this is an overstatement, there is no doubt that often each has major complaints about the other's performance or exercise of authority. Common administrative complaints are that applied anthropologists want too much time for a specific research job, that they define research problems more broadly than administrators feel necessary, that they are unable or unwilling to put research findings in a form administrators and technical specialists can easily understand, that they are too slow in providing information, that they sympathize with members of the target group but are intolerant of the personnel of the innovating organization, and that they want too much time to write for their anthropological peers. Anthropologists, in turn, frequently complain that applied assignments do not permit them sufficient time for really good research, that they are used too often as trouble-shooters, pulled from one task and directed to another when a crisis arises, and that they are not given sufficient time to prepare full and detailed studies, of use to both administrators and professional colleagues.

Obviously, if applied anthropology is to achieve full maturity, the problem of mutually satisfying relationships between anthropologists and the members of goal-oriented bureaucracies must be resolved. In searching for this resolution, we must remember that when mutual dissatisfaction exists between anthropologists and administrators, it usually is not because either or both are willful or headstrong or obstinate. Rather, as I have suggested previously (Foster 1961; 1962, Chapter 12), it is because each belongs to a distinct professional subculture, with very different concepts of roles, of methods of work, of values and goals. Each, to a greater extent than he realizes, is ethnocentric, assuming that the norms governing the practices within his field are not only correct and desirable but also fairly obvious to everyone else. Each assumes there can be no reasonable disagreement with these norms.

The subcultural "chasm" that separates anthropologists (and most other university based scientists) from personnel in fields such as health, medicine, administration, agriculture, and community development can be seen more clearly if we distinguish between a *discipline* and a *profession*. Anthropologists belong to an academic and scientific discipline, characterized by the assumption that the search for new knowledge represents the highest value. Conceptions of proper roles, of means, ends, objectives, and ethics are inculcated in anthropologists during their formal training and are ingrained in their thinking through the practice of their discipline. As highly trained specialists, anthropologists hope to do the things best calculated, within the limits of their ability, to earn them the approbation of their colleagues in anthropology and closely related fields.

In contrast, planners and administrators belong to professions normally characterized by the assumption that the achievement of organizational goals represents the highest value. In doing good professional work, these specialists draw upon the scientific knowledge of a number of disciplines, as well as that of the professions, collating this knowledge to produce plans which, when enacted, will result in the solution of the problems with which their organizations are charged. Conceptions of proper professional roles, and of means, ends, and ethics, are also inculcated in planners and administrators during their professional training and ingrained in them through practice. Professional practice reflects rather more explicit value judgments than does the work of research scientists: health is better than illness; more agricultural production is preferable to less; dependent peoples must be governed.

Differing Role Expectations. Since academic disciplines stress theoretical research, while professional work stresses goal-directed and problem-solving action, it is natural that the members of the two groups have different expectations about their proper role behavior. Usually members of the two groups do not realize how very different these role assumptions are until they find themselves in harness in a common project. Consequently, when each is to some extent forced out of his subcultural mold and required to modify his role expectations and behavior, a degree of frustration and puzzlement is apt to result.

But why should modification in role playing be so painful? Why should members of disciplines and of professions find it difficult to work in ways different from those they have known in the past, and to substitute, at least partially, the values of other fields for their own? Why should such changes not be an exciting challenge rather than being discomforting? For some people, of course, changing occupations or modifying roles *is* a challenge; it is gratifying to know that one can compete in new fields, and do worthwhile work. Yet for most anthropologists, at least, significant and permanent modifications in their views about the anthropological role are not satisfying. The reasons for this, and the reasons for frequent administrative dissatisfaction with the attitude of the anthropologist, can be seen from an examination of the ego-gratifying mechanisms of the two fields.

Role Performance Evaluation. In every field, the ultimate evaluation of performance is made by members of that field. That is, both anthropologists and administrators are, in the first instance, judged and appraised by their peers. An anthropologist is considered to be a leader in his field not because of what an administrator thinks of his work, not because he draws large classes, but because the cumulative evaluation of his fellow anthropologists is that he merits distinction. Conversely, however much an anthropologist may be impressed by the performance of an administrator in a program to which he is attached, this evaluation — while doubtless gratifying to the administrator, if he knows about it — is not what is most meaningful to him. Recognition of distinction can, in most cases, come to him only from fellow administrators.

In other words, anthropologists (and members of other academic disciplines) and administrators (and planners and technical experts) play to different galleries. Not only are the galleries distinct, but *what is seen as good role performance* in the two fields is distinct. In anthropology, as in other academic disciplines, the scientist is judged ultimately by the quality of his research and of his contributions to basic theory. Ability, of course, is basic to the best research, but alone it is insufficient. The able anthropologist must have an institutional base that provides him with the environment — the time, assistance, and funds — he needs to realize his basic potential. Also important for most anthropologists is contact with colleagues and students with similar knowledge and interests. With these sounding boards, new ideas, hunches, and hypotheses can be tried out informally and, through the feedback process that accompanies good teaching and good relationships with colleagues, ideas are refined and reworked until they can be prepared for publication.

It is hard to overemphasize the importance of a good environmental setting for the best role performance in anthropology: a combination of the stimulation that comes from teaching, from discussions with colleagues, and from freedom to pick research topics, with time to carry out research and, especially important, time to write up in detail the results of scientific research. A big university, obviously, is seen by most anthropologists as most nearly the ideal environment in which to perform their role.

In professional work, people are judged on the basis of criteria quite distinct from those of the university based scientist. Their skill in carrying out the tasks expected of them in their professional roles, of reaching goals toward which their efforts are directed, of sensing and reacting correctly to political imperatives, and of acting with brilliance and insight in decision making all determine the evaluation made of their performance. Publications and new hypotheses, while not totally lacking in significance, carry far less weight in this evaluation than in an academic discipline.

Whatever the basis for evaluation of a particular professional performance, it should be noted that, in those action settings in which anthropologists have worked, program administrators usually do not see their ability to do basic research and to publish results as a part of good role performance. Consequently, innovating organizations normally are not set up to give the freedom and writing time anthropologists consider essential for their best work. A full-time applied anthropological career rarely provides the institutional environment in which the best anthropological performances can be executed.

To recapitulate, both anthropologists and administrators, and other professionals as well, strive toward what they feel to be good role performance, in order to earn the recognition in their fields that they desire. Obviously, if either a professional specialist or an anthropologist is required to spend a great deal of time in work which does not lead toward this goal, he is not going to be very happy. Probably, in fact, he will not engage in the activity at all. An anthropologist working on an applied assignment certainly takes satisfaction in knowing that administrators and technical experts — his immediate colleagues — feel he is making an important contribution to program goals. But this approbation alone is not enough to keep an anthropologist happy for long. If he already has an established reputation, he can afford the luxury of a summer, or even one or two years, in an applied assignment, gambling that the insights and knowledge he acquires from this experience will, in the long run, be valuable to him. A young man, just starting the ladder to success, must think longer. He must weigh the advantages of a rich applied experience against the likelihood that he will not have the publication record he needs for advancement, if he returns to academic work. For him, ability to please nonacademic personnel in the action organization is satisfying, but does not lead to the most rapid progress in his chosen field.

SATISFACTORY WORKING RELATIONSHIPS

We now turn from general points about the problems of cooperation between anthropologists and administrators to consider the conditions which must exist if an anthropologist is to be reasonably happy in an applied assignment. There are, it seems to me, at least three such conditions:

1. Both anthropologists and administrators of innovating organizations must appreciate their differing concepts of good role performance, and each must be willing to accommodate himself in some degree so that a mutually satisfying compromise about the anthropologist's duties can be worked out.
2. Based on an understanding of the problems of role performance, a clear definition of the tasks of the anthropologist in an action program must be agreed upon before work begins.
3. This definition must include a clearly defined administrative relationship between the anthropologist and the innovating bureaucracy.

Recognition of Differing Roles. Before an anthropologist accepts an applied assignment he should make sure he knows what is expected of him and what the conditions of the proposed work will be. Only if he is in basic sympathy with the goals of the organization, and can work for it enthusiastically and without reservation, can he accept an assignment honestly. At the same time, he must recognize that in any bureaucracy absolute guarantees about conditions of work, about research freedom, and about time limits can never be given. He owes it to himself to learn the inherent limitations and handicaps under which bureaucracies labor, and over which even the most generous administrators do not have absolute control, since they are themselves limited in their courses and degrees of action. The anthropologist must not assume the administrator is all powerful; he must see him as another human being, interested in achieving goals he feels to be important, circumscribed in his ability to do so by staff and budgetary problems and by his need to make a plausible case for his program in his annual budget proposal.

The administrator must, within the limits permitted him, create working conditions acceptable to anthropologists. He must recognize that this will mean a freedom of action (and perhaps a lack of the time-clock sense) normally not encouraged in administrative organizations. He must accept the fact that the anthropologist's satisfaction from his work is based on criteria quite distinct from those of most of his other staff members and that, if the anthropologist cannot meet the canons of good anthropological role performance to a reasonable extent, he will probably be of slight value to the program. Above all, an administrator must resist the tendency to use the anthropologist as a trouble-shooter, pulling him off one project before work is fairly under way to assign him to a newer crisis. Nothing is so destructive of morale, not to say good research, as this bureaucratic habit of turning staff talent from one assignment to another on the spur of the moment.

The Anthropologist's Role in Action Programs. Anthropologists' views on proper roles in action programs cover a wide spectrum. Polar points set the limits. Many anthropologists see their role to be that of providing "technical information." That is, they gather data on the topic of concern to the administrator, explain how it fits into wider culture patterns, and predict, as best they can, the results of alternative courses of action open to the administrator. With this strict view of role, the anthropologist does not recommend courses of action. The opposite concept of role ranges from anthropologists' recommending how to meet a problem to their occupying formal administrative posts, in which they themselves may implement the action they feel to be indicated.

Godfrey Wilson, in a paper that commanded wide assent when it appeared, argued the first position. "The social anthropologist," he wrote, "cannot as a scientist, judge of good and evil, but only of objective social fact and its implications . . ." (Wilson 1940:45). Since the answers to the problems toward which innovating organizations direct their efforts depend on varying concepts of human welfare, which are matters of opinion and not science, the anthropologist cannot give "scientific" answers, and he should not try. "The qualities and values of life run like water through the scientific net, which catches only the pebbles of objective fact and the branching twigs of necessary implication" (*ibid.*:46). Hence, supplying "technical information," which explains to the administrator the nature of the situations with which he deals, is the only legitimate role of the anthropologist.

Although this view was expressed more than a generation ago, it still reflects the opinion of many anthropologists. It is, however, difficult to adhere to such rigid restrictions. Wilson himself, in the article in which he argues for a "technical information" role, describes a case on which he worked among the Nyakyusa of southern Tanganyika. The question had to do with ownership rights to coffee trees (the cultivation of which had recently been introduced) when the man who had planted a grove moved away. Wilson pointed out to the district officer that bananas, a traditional crop, raised a similar question, and he suggested that the native rules applied to banana tree ownership might serve as a basis for ones on coffee trees, modifying the traditional rule so that the planter, if he moved away, would nevertheless receive a percentage of the crop (*ibid.*:51). Wilson did not simply inform the district office of traditional ownership concepts; he went beyond this to recommend a policy which he thought would work.

The late S. F. Nadel took a position which seems to me more realistic. He argued that an anthropologist, as a scientist, ". . . is bound to make judgements on the nature of society and on the purposes of human behaviour; as a critic or perhaps planner of policy he merely applies the same kind of judgement to problems of which he happens to have cognizance as a citizen or social being" (Nadel 1951:55). Anthropologists can, of course, leave the drawing of conclusions to others, but Nadel felt that the anthropologist, because of his intimate knowledge of the situation, is often the one best suited to draw them. Anthropologists will err at times, said Nadel, "But blunders are always being committed — often by men insensible of the premises from which they argue and ignorant about the nature of the processes they attempt to influence or better. The blunders of anthropologists will be 'better' blunders" (*ibid.*:55).

Although most contemporary anthropologists feel it is unwise for them to combine administrative and research assignments, few if any applied anthropologists stick to the "technical information only" position popular in an earlier period and enunciated by Wilson. Most believe the anthropologist has the knowledge, the right, and the responsibility to express his views as to the best solutions to problems on which he has worked.

Administrative Relationships. In examining the history of applied anthropology, we find at least four basic types of relationships between anthropologists and innovating organizations: (1) no formal administrative tie; (2) the anthropologist as consultant; (3) direct hire of the anthropologist by such an organization; and (4) the anthropologist as administrator. We will examine each of these relationships.

1. No Formal Administrative Tie. As Lantis pointed out many years ago, a good deal of what passes for applied anthropology is, in fact, not applied work at all. "Merely observing and recording how a mining village in the United States reacts to a new administrative program or works out its problems is just cultural anthropology, like the recording of cultural processes in a Chinese village or any other locality where the anthropologist may go to observe and record" (Lantis 1945:20). By these criteria, and I agree with them, a relatively small part of the research reported in *Human Organization*, the journal of the Society for Applied Anthropology, is applied work.

Several years ago I analyzed the results of the CREFAL community development program in Tzintzuntzan (Foster 1967a: Chapter 17). My work was not applied anthropology; it was simply part of a more general analysis of the processes of change in the village. *If* my observations had been used by CREFAL personnel in evaluating its program, or *if* they had been used as justification for program modification, or *if* I had been called in by CREFAL as a consultant to discuss program improvements, then my work would have become applied anthropology. The data certainly are pertinent to CREFAL's operations, but until and unless specific use is made of them, the analysis is nothing more than straightforward social anthropology.

The fact is that however useful anthropological analysis may be to action programs, usually it is very little used unless the anthropologist himself has a formal tie to the organization. "The essential difficulty," as Barnett has pointed out, ". . . is that the research specialist is regarded as a stranger, often as an interloper, by regular government officials. He has no status within their organization, so his views can be treated like those of any other outside observer or critic" (Barnett 1956:172). Even at best, Barnett goes on to note, reports and memoranda are ignored or miss their target. "This is the more certain to happen to a technical advisor who operates entirely on his own initiative, independently deciding what should be explored and not being informed or appealed to on matters which the administration regards as problems" (*ibid.*:172). For all practical purposes, we can discount as applied anthropology research and evaluation not in some way tied to an innovating bureaucracy.

2. Consultant. Anthropologists increasingly are used today by government, by the United Nations, and by private organizations, as short- and long-term consultants. Short-term consultants are called away from their usual teaching and research assignments for one or a few days of meetings to consider problems of concern to a bureaucracy. No research is done; the anthropologist, reasoning from past experience and similar instances, simply advances

his ideas as to the factors pertinent to the situation and, depending on the situation, makes recommendations for follow-up work.

It is important to distinguish between the manifest and the latent functions of anthropological consultants. Because they lack full knowledge of the problems on which they are advising, short-term consultants seem to me usually to have rather limited value. That is, their manifest function, to bring specialized knowledge to bear on a problem, is not always realized. At the same time, their latent function may be considerable, for often they are validating or symbolically approving the decisions already made by the responsible administrator. The administrator, by calling in presumably competent judges to view his program and to make recommendations, is forestalling criticism of his acts. His position obviously is strengthened if he can point to recognized authorities who have consulted with him and approved what he has done or proposed to do (and anthropologists, by and large, do in fact place their stamps of approval on programs on which they consult). The administrator, by making liberal use of consultants, shows that he has done everything he can be expected to do in order to make sure his decisions are sound. If things work out well, he enhances his reputation as an able administrator; if they do not, he can share the blame with specialists and point to circumstances beyond his control.

Long-term consultants are little different from direct hire employees, described in the following paragraphs.

3. Direct Hire. An innovating organization sometimes hires anthropologists in the same way it acquires other personnel. Such employment, which may last from a number of months to several years, gives time for original research as well as for the opportunity to come to know technical specialists as friends and professional colleagues. Usually this is the most effective relationship, in spite of its drawbacks. A most important argument for a formal association is that only in this way can the anthropologist be a participant observer in the bureaucratic subculture which, as we have seen, is a part of his research interest. In an applied pro-

gram, an outsider usually cannot gain the full confidence of the personnel of an innovating organization, convince them that he has no ulterior motives, and assure them that their interests are also his. But when he is a formal member of a bureaucracy, he rubs shoulders with other specialists, participates in staff meetings, sees the handicaps under which bureaucrats labor, and becomes committed to their practical as well as his own scientific goals. Under these conditions he is in a position to analyze the bureaucracy effectively, to understand how its structure, operations, and premises bear upon the success or failure of its programs.

In studying a tribe or peasant community, an anthropologist, as a consequence of being close to the people over a long period of time, usually identifies with the people, feels sympathy and friendship for them, and is concerned for their welfare. The same psychological process usually occurs through close association with a bureaucratic subculture. This is not to say the anthropologist loves all bureaucrats any more than he loves all the people of the peasant village he has come to know well. It does mean that a genuine identification with the bureaucratic community, an understanding of its problems and limitations, and a liking for a great many of its people puts the anthropologist in a strong position from which to weigh all the factors involved in a change situation and to make meaningful recommendations.

Administrators at least have long recognized the importance of this relationship. A good many years ago Lord Hailey wrote, "I suggest that it should be recognized that acquaintance with the practical problems of colonial development is an essential preparation for undertaking social or anthropological research in the colonial field" (Hailey 1944:15). And later he added, "it may be suggested that Governments are likely to derive the greatest advantage from inquiries undertaken by anthropologists in close association with their own technical or Administrative Officers" (Hailey 1957:61).

Evans-Pritchard, whose general position on applied anthropology can only be described as extremely conservative, fully appreciates the importance of a close relationship: "It is important that the anthropologist who acts as adviser, or consultant, to an administration should be a full member of it. He cannot advise the administration on the bearing of their legal, educational, economic, and other social programmes on native life unless he knows the bureaucratic machinery from the inside, has full access to all government documents, and meets the heads of departments round the same conference table as an equal. Otherwise he will not be able to see problems in their full administrative context as well as their full anthropological context . . ." (Evans-Pritchard 1946:97).

4. Administrator. Should an anthropologist, in his line of applied work, accept administrative responsibilities? Can anthropological research be carried out by administrators who are trained in anthropological methods? To the latter question, today's answer is "no." Yet it is interesting that at one time the answer was "yes." Rattray, of the Golden Stool incident, was a colonial officer trained in anthropology. He believed that, for the problems of colonial administration in the 1920's, ". . . the best results are likely to be obtained by training as anthropologists, men already possessing some experience of the people, the language, and the country generally, and also of the problems of administration" (Rattray 1923:8). The early and highly successful applied anthropological work in New Guinea carried out by Chinnery and Williams also represents this pattern: professional colonial officers subsequently trained in social anthropology (pages 188–190).

It is an interesting coincidence that some of the last applied anthropological research in a colonial setting carried out by an administrator trained in anthropology also took place in New Guinea, in this case the western part controlled, prior to its transfer to Indonesia, by the Netherlands. Dr. J. W. Schoorl, the anthropologist-administrator, has described a six-month assignment carried out in 1954 among the primitive Muyu of what is now West Irian, and his experiences well illustrate the advantages and disadvantages of his dual role. Schoorl had been with the New

Guinea administration for two years when he was assigned by
Governor van Baal, himself a distinguished anthropologist, to
make studies that would permit the establishment of an improved
administrative system, and when he completed his research he
was appointed administrator of the Muyu subdivision.

Arguing in favor of the anthropologist-administrator doing this
type of investigation, Schoorl points out that "All administrative
work has to take place within a framework of existing ideas, traditions, laws and regulations and available means." By selecting an
administrative officer to do the research himself, there was no
question but that the officer would be sensitive to the problems of
colonial administration, and that his recommendations would fit
the existing administrative framework. Schoorl correctly points
out that an anthropologist unfamiliar with administration would
work less rapidly. Time always has been a critical factor in colonial administration: "Administrative work continues even if no
detailed information is available and often, unfortunately, decisions have to be made on the basis of insufficient knowledge"
(Schoorl 1967:173).

As an anthropologist, Schoorl recognized that he must be entirely free of administrative obligations while doing research. Unfortunately, he found, "Administrators on the whole are not very
sensitive to the desirability for the investigator to dissociate himself as much as possible from the authorities" (*ibid.*, 178), and
only Governor van Baal's intervention made it possible for him to
have the desired autonomy. Even then he was not able entirely to
dissociate himself from administration, since local officials, missionaries, and school teachers in the area knew his official post,
and treated him accordingly. This was not, however, without advantages, since "As a former colleague I enjoyed the complete
confidence of the administrative officials in the district," which facilitated acquisition of some types of data (*ibid.*, 178). On balance, Schoorl seems not to have felt unduly handicapped by his
dual role.

The greatest dangers associated with a professional administrator doing anthropological research appear, in the eyes of Schoorl,

to lie in a different direction. First, he may have difficulties in detaching his mental processes from the administrative context, and thus acquiring the flexibility that will permit him to see new possibilities. Second, the administrator-anthropologist inevitably "is a member of a bureaucratic organization and as such is involved, whether consciously or unconsciously, in the competition for higher posts. A temporary assignment outside the actual administrative apparatus does not mean that the influence of this competition is altogether absent" (*ibid.*, 174). The problem, of course, is objectivity. When a man is competing within an administrative rather than an anthropological hierarchy, will his professional aspirations be reflected in his reports and recommendations? Will he dare risk making recommendations which are highly critical of administration and which may involve, if carried out, major modifications in prevailing attitudes and practices? Most people are reluctant to displease their administrative superiors. Schoorl feels that the academic anthropologist is not entirely free of these subtle pressures, but that they are less likely to affect his work, since his future success is not tied to administration.

Today the question of the anthropological administrator's place in colonial administration is moot, since the system is dead, and the conditions that permitted this type of applied anthropology no longer exist. Even were the colonial system still alive, it seems unlikely that much sound research could be carried out by administrators with a year or two of anthropological training. Sound preparation in social anthropology takes much longer than it did fifty years ago: usually five graduate years is a minimum. Just as it is unreasonable to expect an anthropologist to become a skilled animal husbandman or plant geneticist in order to work in a technical aid program, so it is unreasonable today to expect a nonanthropologist, a specialist in his own field, to do the work an anthropologist is trained to do.

This leaves unanswered the question of how far into administration an anthropologist may venture. The answer, of course, depends on temperament and opportunity. In general, American experience indicates that the anthropologist who expects to do research on the group toward whom a program is directed is best advised to avoid administrative assignments. First, there is hardly time both to do research and to administer. Second, an administrator must make decisions which sometimes will be unpopular. If a research anthropologist is the one to make such decisions, his utility in gathering data is in large part destroyed; he simply cannot maintain the type of rapport with informants that is essential for the best research. As Barnett puts it, "No matter how competent and well-intentioned an administrator-anthropologist may be, he is placed in an almost impossible position because of the antithesis embodied in his dual role. He cannot enforce a rule and at the same time inquire into reactions to it with the hope of getting genuine responses. His status as a power figure seldom fails to create a psychological gap which manifests itself in an attitude of reserve, at least on the part of the governed" (Barnett 1956:176).

On the other hand, I see no reason why an anthropologist should not function as an administrator, if he so wishes, and if it is recognized that he is an administrator who simply happens to have had anthropological training, or who for a specific period is acting as an administrator rather than as a research anthropologist. A very few American anthropologists have made careers of administration, sacrificing in large measure the pleasures of research for the satisfactions that come from administrative accomplishments. Others, of whom Gladwin is perhaps the best example, have served successfully in administrative capacities after they have, through traditional research, come to know well the people and the problems involved. Gladwin's Micronesian research provided him with knowledge of the language and culture of the peoples of Truk and surrounding islands. Subsequently, as Native Affairs Officer, he was responsible to the commanding officer of the local area, with administrative (rather than research) activities in the field of political and economic affairs. Gladwin felt that, as an anthropologist, he was better prepared than anyone else to act on political and economic affairs, because of his intimate knowledge of them. He found that, as an administrator, he had to rely on the work of other anthropologists, but that there were compensations. Above all he felt that in implementing his own decisions he was sticking his neck out "in the best American tradition." If he failed, his failure would be weighed against other successes; someone else's failures, based on anthropological recommendations, would not be used to discredit anthropology. He concluded that "If the job is worth doing, the anthropologist must do it himself" (Gladwin 1956:64–65).

Most anthropologists do not go this far, simply because they find that administrative frustrations outweigh satisfactions, and that sound research is usually a more appealing alternative. At the same time we must recognize that there is nothing inherently wrong with an anthropologist serving as administrator, if conditions are propitious.

The Outside-Insider. Eventually, a fully developed subdiscipline of applied anthropology will come into being. Some anthropologists, because of temperament and other reasons, will seek careers in which their primary associations will be not with universities but with goal-oriented bureaucracies. But this pattern may not develop for a good many years. If the academic environment, with its stimulation from colleagues and students, its pattern of varied activities, from teaching to research to writing, is as important as I think it is, perhaps the attempt should be made to keep it as a part of the background of applied anthropologists. Srinivas, speaking of the problems of applied social science research in developing countries, correctly points out that "Over the years, sociologists employed by the government are likely to find their expertise blunted and out of date, just as their bureaucratic sense is likely to become keener" (Srinivas 1966:161). He proposes that career applied social scientists as well as government might benefit if the former periodically spent a few months in universities, attending refresher courses and catching up with late developments. This has been suggested and tried in the United States, but in general, although the idea is meritorious, it works out rather poorly in practice.

An opposite tack, which I personally prefer, is to facilitate the use of university anthropologists in action programs by permitting longer leaves of absence (at least two years on occasion) without academic penalty. Two-year periods allow time to become acquainted with the innovating organization (particularly if the anthropologist has had prior experience in similar settings), and time to do good research and to communicate significant data by memoranda and in staff meetings to program administrators and technical experts. In two years, a knowledgeable anthropologist can contribute to an action program a great many of the things program personnel want. By retreating to his university department, and by using summer vacations and sabbatical leaves, the anthropologist can then prepare the longer, more thoughtful reports that will be of interest to his colleagues. Most bureaucracies simply cannot give the anthropologist the time he needs for this kind of writing, and perhaps they should not attempt to do so. A further advantage of the "outside-insider" is that he provides a means of passing applied research results to students, of acquainting them with a wider spectrum of anthropological activities than would otherwise be possible. If applied anthropology were to become the exclusive domain of non-teaching applied anthropologists, much of value might be lost to students and to the field at large.

Srinivas also sees merit in this approach. "Perhaps those sociologists most useful to committees are the ones who have had some experience of how the development agencies of the government work, and how these agencies actually collect their data. The employment in government of academic sociologists for short periods, or for particular assignments, may be desirable from several points of view. It gives the sociologists inside knowledge of how policies are implemented at various levels of government, and of the relations between officials and the people. In other words, it would be a kind of 'field experience' of development for them" (*ibid.*:162). Whether such an arrangement will prove to be the best in the long run, we cannot yet tell. For a number of years, at least, we can expect academic anthropologists to continue to play the major role in applied work.

173

THE QUESTION OF ETHICS

In both applied and traditional academic research the anthropologist is much concerned with the moral implications of his actions. Although in applied work the ethical problems often are accentuated, the underlying rule of behavior followed by all anthropologists is the same: respect confidences. In adhering to this rule, anthropologists simply follow the lead of ministers and priests, lawyers, physicians, and others who are privy to confidential information and who must ensure that this information is used only in ways which will not injure those who gave it. It is essential to anthropologists in both applied and theoretical research that informants feel secure in the knowledge that their confidences will not be betrayed, and that they can speak freely to the researcher. And, to the non-anthropologist, it is frequently a source of amazement that informants will reveal so much that is highly intimate and confidential.

Ethics in Traditional Research. This informal code of ethics and the sense of responsibility that has characterized anthropological research from its earliest days have worked amazingly well. I can think of no instances involving tribal or peasant peoples in which injudicious use of research data has harmed the peoples concerned, either in fact or in their sensibilities. As more and more the anthropologist has studied literate peoples, and has turned his attention to his own society, he has exercised greater caution in revealing individual, and even group, identities. First Muncie became "Middletown," to disguise its identity, and then Tepoztlán became "Azteca." Although aggrieved literate groups occasionally complain about how an anthropologist has described them, in general members of the discipline have a rather remarkable record of keeping out of serious trouble and protecting the interests of the people with whom they work. It is rare for an anthropologist to be unable to return to a community he has described. In most instances, he is welcomed back with open arms. People are delighted to know he has so enjoyed a former stay with them that he wishes to return.

The circumstances that promote this happy state of affairs are dual. First, normally the anthropologist gives no thought to active intervention in the lives of the people studied. He is not concerned with changing their ways. In fact, this is usually the last thing he wants to do. Hence, no question arises as to social and economic ends, and as to what would be good and what would be bad for the people. And second, as pointed out in the model describing applied in relation to theoretical anthropology, the theoretical anthropologist exercises absolute control over his data. He is the one who decides how they are to be used, what is to be said, and what is to be filed away for possible future use. He does not say in print everything he knows, or feels is pertinent to an argument. And, since the theoretical anthropologist is aware that the final responsibility for making his knowledge public rests on his shoulders alone, he does not have to worry about the possible indiscretions of other well-meaning people who, with rights over his data, may feel no qualms about using them in the pursuance of their goals. Hence, the combination of control over research data and the lack of interest in changing people reduces the ethical problems of theoretical anthropology, in most instances, to caution in revealing confidences.

Ethics in Applied Research. In applied settings the magnitude of the ethical problem increases. First, there is the basic philosophical question of who, if anyone, has the right to intervene, in a position of authority and dominance, in the lives of others. And second, there is the question of who decides, and on the basis of what evidence, what is good for the members of a target group. These are questions science cannot answer. Yet science does have a basic role in seeking answers, for it can provide the hard data which should be a part of the knowledge of all those who, on political, social, and philosophical grounds, do seek such answers.

About the first question — who, if anyone, has the right to intervene in the lives of others — I take for granted that in a complex society and a complex world it is utopian and unrealistic to assume that people can live without intervention. My whole life and the lives of all readers of this book have been marked by intervention by parents, by school authorities, by government, by health departments. With much of what they have done, I agree; with some, I do not. The problem, then, is not: can or ought people to have absolute freedom to accept or reject all authority and outside influences that result in changes in traditional ways? The question is: how can the exercise of such authority be structured to minimize injustice and to maximize individual freedom? Most of us probably feel that the best answer is found in the democratic process, which gives us the right *and* the obligation to inform ourselves as best we can on all pertinent issues, to express our beliefs, and to work toward those goals we feel to be most productive of a healthy society.

The anthropologist, then, like every other citizen of a democracy, has the right and the duty to express himself on the fundamental issues of our times. Quite naturally, his specialized anthropological knowledge will be instrumental in determining the position he takes. He cannot justify this position as scientific, objective, and value-free. But he can justify it as an informed, thoughtful, considered position which, on many problems such as race relations and social aspects of development, may be more realistic than the positions of other persons whose scientific knowledge of underlying factors may be less extensive.

Working in applied settings, the anthropologist is associated with bureaucracies which have made decisions about ends; that is the reason for their being. The anthropologist cannot avoid identification with these ends, even though in all likelihood he had nothing to do with determining them. Some anthropologists argue that, if the anthropologist restricts his role to giving technical information, he avoids the issue of the ethics of intervention. This, I think, is not a valid argument. In accepting an applied assignment, the anthropologist also accepts an ethical responsibility of a type quite distinct from that characterizing his field at large: he must decide whether he is sympathetic, at least generally, with the methods and goals of the organization with which he will work, and whether he believes that, as a consequence of his participation, these goals will be reached more easily, or the answers worked out will be more nearly consonant with the needs of the people concerned. If the answer is no, or if there are grave doubts, the anthropologist should refuse such work. He cannot avoid responsibility by saying that his role is only to supply technical information, and that the responsibility of deciding how such information should be used rests with other experts.

We must remember that, in an applied program, the anthropologist usually controls neither his data nor the ends for which they are used. He has the ethical responsibility to make available to the bureaucracy with which he works a large part of the results of his research; that is why he is there. But, just as in his own writing he does not say all he knows, so in an applied setting he does not necessarily reveal all he has learned. The same discretionary latitude must prevail in the two situations. Qualitatively, however, there is a difference. In applied work, the anthropologist knows that unskillful or perhaps overambitious administrators and technical experts will have access to data which can be used in many ways, which may prejudice the lives of informants, and which, improperly used, may result in poor programs. One reason I feel an applied anthropologist must have close contact with operations personnel is so that he may exercise, to the greatest degree possible, continuing control over the use of data, be able to spot possible misuse in time to call a halt, and generally exercise a restraining influence.

In most of the applied programs in which I have worked, I have been in basic sympathy with program goals and have felt no major conflicts in associating myself with them. About the broad objectives of most technical aid programs, there is little question. The problems are in how they are to be carried out. In this, I think, lies the real contribution by the anthropologist. His research often makes possible a better program, one that fits the needs and potentials of the recipient peoples. I have seen some programs with which I would not wish to be associated, but I see no major ethical conflict with a majority of today's technical aid programs.

Moral Doubts. In other periods a major conflict has existed. This was particularly true in colonial Africa, the site of some of the earliest and most successful applied anthropology — successful at least from the standpoint of administrators and anthropologists. Ultimately, British anthropologists came to have serious doubts as to the ethical implications of their work, and for this reason a great many not only withdrew, but also became active critics of applied work, which, of course, they continued to see largely in the outmoded terms of the administration of dependent peoples. Nadel tells how his eyes were opened when, after experience in Nigeria, and strongly attracted to the ideals of Indirect Rule, he addressed an academic meeting in London and described the role anthropology could play in furthering this system. "At the end of the talk a number of West African students in the audience violently attacked me, all my fellow-workers in that field, and indeed the whole of anthropology. They accused us of playing into the hands of reactionary administrators and of lending the sanction of science to a policy meant to 'keep the African down'" (Nadel 1953:13). Obviously, the perfecting of Indirect Rule was not consistent with the goals of African nationalism.

This fundamental conflict was recognized by Firth when he wrote, "If the anthropologist is asked to help in making a policy of Colonial rule more efficient, is this with the ultimate object of fitting the people for self-government, with freedom of choice as to the form of political institutions that they may finally desire, or is it with the aim of simply getting a more cohesive community, with law and order better kept, taxes paid more promptly, and social services more efficiently carried out, all to remain within the framework of an Imperial system?" (Firth 1958:164–165). The conviction that the latter philosophy characterized colonial rule in the immediate postwar years seems to explain British disenchantment with applied work.

Codes of Ethics. The ethical problem in applied anthropology is important, always present, but by no means insuperable. If the anthropologist will exercise the same good judgment and caution that traditionally have characterized his field research, and apply the same standard of personal ethics, he should encounter no major doubts. He should participate only in those projects in which he feels morally comfortable, and he should withdraw from any in which he discovers policies or practices he cannot accept. Basing his opinions on science as well as on personal philosophy, the anthropologist in goal-oriented programs should speak out as a citizen and actively work toward realization of the ends he feels to be justified. In the pursuit of these ends, he has both an informal and a formal code of ethics to guide him. The informal code is, of course, personal; it is the precise statement which the individual works out to guide his conduct in a specific situation. The formal code is the official position of the Society for Applied Anthropology.

An Informal Code. The stand taken by the late Allan Holmberg and his colleagues in the Cornell Peru Vicos Project illustrates an informal code of ethics which to me seems highly humane and reasonable: "While it is impossible here to consider all of the facets of the value problem, I would like simply to state this with respect to our work at Vicos: we took a value stand, one that has since been defined in great detail: we were concerned with helping the Vicosiños to transform the hacienda on which they now live in a dependent and submissive state into a 'just, peaceable, morally and intellectually progressive community of . . . responsible men and women.' While, of course, no such value position can ever be justified scientifically, we — and many Vicosiños — believe these to be good and desirable ends. Actually, beyond a clear statement of one's value position, little further need be said about the value problem" (Holmberg 1955:25).

A Formal Code. As long ago as 1946 the Society for Applied Anthropology recognized the need for a formal code of ethics, to guide its members in their applied work and to remind them continually of the implications of action work. The most recent statement on ethics of the Society, adopted in 1963, follows:

An applied anthropologist may not undertake to act professionally with or without remuneration, in any situation where he cannot honor all of the following responsibilities within the limit of the foreseeable effects of his action. When these responsibilities are in conflict, he must insist on a redefinition of the terms of his employment. If the conflict cannot be resolved, or if he has good reason to suspect that the results of his work will be used in a manner harmful to the interests of his fellow men or of science, he must decline to make his services available.

To Science he has the responsibility of avoiding any actions or recommendations that will impede the advancement of scientific knowledge. In the wake of his own studies he must undertake to leave a hospitable climate for future study. With due regard to his other responsibilities as set forth here, he should undertake to make data and findings available for scientific purposes. He should not represent hypotheses or personal opinions as scientifically validated principles.

To his fellow men he owes respect for [their] dignity and general well-being. He may not recommend any course of action on behalf of his client's interests, when the lives, well-being, dignity, and self-respect of others are likely to be adversely affected, without adequate provisions being made to insure that there will be a minimum of such effect and that the net effect will in the long run be more beneficial than if no action were taken at all. He must take the greatest care to protect his informants, especially in the aspects of confidence which his informants may not be able to stipulate for themselves.

To his clients he must make no promises nor may he encourage any expectations that he cannot reasonably hope to fulfill. He must give them the best of his scientific knowledge and skill. He must consider their specific goals in the light of their general interests and welfare. He must establish a clear understanding with each client as to the nature of his responsibilities to his client, to science, and to his fellow men" (Anonymous 1963–1964).

If standards similar to those here stated are followed in applied anthropological work, the anthropologist need not fear that he can be criticized on ethical grounds, nor that he is acting in a way unbecoming a scientist and a citizen.

CHAPTER 9   the development of
applied anthropology

Science and scientific trends are no exception to the rule that a contemporary picture is better understood if its history is known. This is certainly true of applied anthropology, whose current forms and place within the broad discipline can be fully appreciated only with knowledge of the several stages of its development. Although significant applied anthropological work has been done and is being done in many countries, the combined British and American experiences in this field are preeminent for size, geographical range, and variety of activities. In this final chapter primary attention is therefore devoted to the history of the field in these two countries. In priority Britain rightfully comes first, since both the recognition of the practical value of anthropology, and the formal employment of applied anthropologists, first occurred in that country.

Early British Applied Anthropology. Contrary to what many anthropologists believe — namely, that applied anthropology is a relatively late phenomenon, and that in its beginnings anthropology was unconcerned with contemporary problems — the practical value of anthropology has been taken for granted since the subject's earliest days. In the middle of the last century Englishmen of science and letters, concerned with the problems of slavery, the treatment of aborigines in the empire, and colonial administration, turned to anthropology to find answers and, it must be confessed, to justify their stands.

Reining has skillfully summarized this "lost period" of applied anthropological interest of more than a century ago (Reining 1962). He points out that, even as today, there was a division of opinion between research-oriented and action-oriented people. When the Aborigines Protective Society was established in London in 1838, its academic faction wanted to study native peoples to find out how they lived and what they wanted before trying to help them, while its missionary faction wanted to bestow on them immediately the "privileges" of European civilization. Dissatisfied with this action-now philosophy, the academic group seceded in 1843 and formed the Ethnological Society of London. Writing in 1856 in Volume 4 of the *Journal of the Ethnological Society*, Sir B. C. Brodie argued that "Ethnology is now generally recognized as having the strongest claims in our attention, not merely as it tends to gratify the curiosity of those who love to look into Nature's works, but also *as being of great practical importance, especially in this country, whose numerous colonies and extensive commerce bring it into contact with so many varieties of the human species* differing in their physical and moral qualities both from each other and from ourselves" (quoted from Reining 1962:593 — emphasis added).

Twenty years later a large segment of the Ethnological Society in turn seceded to form the Anthropological Society of London which, highly successful for several years, did much to popularize anthropology in its two journals, *The Anthropological Review* and the *Popular Magazine of Anthropology*. The conviction of this society's members that anthropology was a practical subject is clearly indicated in numerous signed and unsigned articles in these journals, such as the following quotation from "Race in Legislation and Political Economy": "It is a most mistaken idea that Anthropology is purely speculative and abstract. It is, on the contrary, more intimately related than any other branch of science to the sympathies of humanity, and, we may add, the utilities and requirements of society. It enters into every question connected with religion, government, commerce, and culture, which are all more or less affected by racial endowment and proclivity" (Anonymous 1866:113).

Unfortunately, the popularity of the Anthropological Society of London was due, in part, at least, to the fact that it was pronouncedly racist. Leading members, such as the president, Dr. James Hunt, argued that science (including phrenology!) proved the Negro to be physically, intellectually, and morally inferior to the European. Although they agreed that the Negro was a man, they felt that "to affirm that a Negro is in every way as good a man as a European, is to deny the historic testimony of five thousand years, seeing that in all that time no Negro nation has ever, either with or without assistance, reached the civilisation, again and again achieved in the great centres of Caucasian culture" (*ibid.*: 119). Mongoloids fared only slightly better: "Their structure, while superior to that of the Negro, is inferior to that of the European. It is less developed. As the type of the Negro is foetal, that of the Mongol is infantile. And in strict accordance with this we find that their government, literature and art are infantile also. They are beardless children, whose life is a task, and whose chief virtue consists in unquestioning obedience" (*ibid.*: 120). It is a measure of European ethnocentrism of the time, and a blot on the name of anthropology, that such ideas could pass for serious science.

Fortunately, the Anthropological Society's extreme position was against the longer-range social and scientific trends of the times, and in 1871 it rejoined the Ethnological Society to form the [Royal] Anthropological Institute of Great Britain and Ireland, which ever since has been the principal British anthropological association. The new organization abandoned all racist propaganda and concerned itself from the beginning with building an orderly and scientific body of anthropological data and theory and with promoting teaching and research. Real academic recognition for anthropology came only in 1883, when E. B. Tylor was appointed Reader in Anthropology at Oxford, and in 1884, when a separate section for anthropology was established in the British Association for the Advancement of Science.

With respectability, anthropology ceased in essence arguing its practical merits, only rarely paying lip service to this justification. In viewing this early phase of anthropology, we are not really speaking of applied anthropology, for no research was done on practical problems. Rather, people interested in anthropology, for good and bad reasons, simply affirmed that the science was practical and that its findings confirmed their prejudices.

Anthropology in Early British Colonial Administration. Real recognition of anthropology's potential in the administration of native peoples was first foreshadowed by W. H. Flower in his Royal Anthropological Institute presidential address in 1884:

> This subject of ethnography . . . is perhaps the most practically important of the various branches of anthropology. Its importance to those who have to rule — and there are few of us now who are not called upon to bear our share of the responsibility of government — can scarcely be over-estimated in an empire like this, the population of which is composed of examples of almost every diversity under which the human body and mind can manifest itself. . . . As it behoves the wise physician not only to study the particular kind of disease under which his patient is suffering, and then to administer the approved remedies for such disease, but also to take into careful account the peculiar idiosyncrasies and inherited tendencies of the individual . . . so is it absolutely necessary for the statesman who would govern successfully, not to look upon human nature in the abstract and endeavour to apply universal rules, but to consider the special moral, intellectual, and social capabilities, wants, and aspirations of each particular race with which he has to deal. A form of government under which one race would live happily and prosperously would to another be the cause of unendurable misery. The remedies

which may be advisable to mitigate the difficulties and disadvantages under which the English artisan classes may suffer in their struggle through life, would be absolutely inapplicable, for instance, to the case of the Egyptian fellaheen" (Flower 1884: 492–493).

In subsequent years, as the British Empire reached full flower, as the import of racial and cultural differences came to be recognized, as good ethnographical reports (often the work of missionaries) began to appear, and as anthropology achieved status as a legitimate science, the idea slowly took form that anthropological knowledge and training would be a most important adjunct in colonial administration. By the turn of the century, thoughtful and practical men in the fields both of colonial administration and of anthropology were well aware of the importance of the cultural dimension in the successful administration of native peoples.

Thus, at the 1896 meeting of the British Association for the Advancement of Science, a resolution was adopted to the effect that the government should establish "a Bureau of Ethnology for Greater Britain, which, by collecting information with regard to the native races within and on the borders of the Empire, will prove of immense value to science and to the Government itself" (Myers 1929:38). Nothing, however, came of this resolution.

Presenting the administrator's point of view, Sir Richard Temple (whose career had included long service in Burma) in 1904 urged the establishment of an "important school of Applied Anthropology" at Cambridge University to train consular and administrative people (Temple 1914:80), and in subsequent lectures he repeatedly stressed the need for colonial administrators to know the culture of the people they governed. Knowledge of the languages, the administration, and the law of the area concerned is not sufficient preparation, he argued. "It is also necessary to know the culture of the people one is dealing with. This is the knowledge that the Schools of Applied Anthropology advocated by myself and others are intended to provide . . ." (*ibid.*: 2).

Although such a school of applied anthropology never was instituted, some of its aims were significantly furthered with the establishment of degree courses in major British universities: the Oxford Diploma in Anthropology in 1905, the Cambridge "Diploma-by-Thesis" in 1908, and the University of London Honors B.Sc. in 1912. By 1923, eleven British universities provided instruction in anthropology (Myers 1929:43).

Institution of degree courses, with the concomitant expansion of teaching, permitted both universities and the Royal Anthropological Institute to urge government to make use of anthropology in the preparation of its civil servants. Thus, in 1909, both Oxford and Cambridge urged the Indian and Colonial Offices to train civil service candidates in ethnology and primitive religion, and in the same year the Royal Anthropological Institute petitioned the government to initiate official training in anthropology of candidates for the Consular and Indian and Colonial Civil Services. Although the government did not act on these representations, future colonial officials in training began to register in anthropology courses in increasing numbers (Temple 1914:26–28).

The First Applied Anthropological Appointments. This trend received a strong boost in 1908 when Sir Reginald Wingate, organizing a civil service for the Anglo-Egyptian Sudan, asked Oxford and Cambridge to provide training so that candidates for service in the Sudan could be required to study anthropology as a part of their basic preparation (Temple 1914:29; Myers 1929:47). This appears to have been the first instance in which a British dependency formally recognized the importance of anthropology as a part of the background of all of its officials. The Sudan went even further and in the following year appointed the distinguished anthropologist C. G. Seligman (already famous for his classic work on the Vedda of Ceylon) to carry out an ethnographic survey of the territory, with the aim of facilitating government operations. In later years, the Sudan government also sponsored the basic research of other anthropologists, including that of

E. E. Evans-Pritchard among the Nuer and S. F. Nadel among the Nuba. The publications which resulted from this support are not applied anthropology in the usual sense, and the Sudan government appears to have felt that scholarly anthropological research was of general value, rather than of immediate practical utility, in the administration and development of that country.

The Sudan, however, was not the first British dependency to make formal use of anthropology in administration. This distinction goes to Nigeria, with the appointment in 1908 of Northcote W. Thomas. As has often been the case in the use of anthropologists in administration, Thomas was called in because of a crisis. Indirect Rule, introduced in northern Nigeria in 1900 by Lord Lugard, was working less well when the pattern was extended to the Western and Southeastern Provinces. Thomas' assignment was to study the Ibo- and Edo-speaking peoples to facilitate the extension of this form of rule (Hailey 1957:54; Forde 1953:845), and he is identified as "Government Anthropologist" on the title page of several major publications on West Africa published before and during World War I. The content of these monographs, however, is standard ethnography, and indicates no orientation distinct from that of other descriptive works of the period. Thomas' applied contributions must therefore have taken the form of office memoranda and conversations with administrative officers in the colonial service.

In 1919, the Union of South Africa government appointed a commission to investigate the need for research on African languages and customs, as a result of which the University of Cape Town set up professorships of anthropology and Bantu ethnology. This led to an even more direct utilization of anthropology in 1925 with the creation of the Ethnological Section of the Native Affairs Department, whose functions were to promote "scientific investigations and research into Bantu ethnology, sociology, philology, and anthropology," and to provide the Department "with the services of an academically trained anthropologist conversant with the ethnological and linguistic side of Native affairs, accurate information in regard to which, it was realised, was likely to prove of the greatest assistance in the smooth and harmonious administration of tribal affairs and in the prevention of friction" (Schapera 1939:97).

In 1920, the Gold Coast (now Ghana) created the post of Government Anthropologist, appointing to it Captain R. S. Rattray, an administrative officer with anthropological training. His Ashanti investigations have already been mentioned in the account of the Golden Stool (pages 16–18). The following year the Nigerian government appointed Dr. C. K. Meek, also an administrative officer with anthropological training, as Census Commissioner in the Northern Provinces, to ensure as great a quantity as possible of ethnographic data in the 1921 census. Data so obtained, together with information from subsequent investigations by Dr. Meek, played a major role in 1927 revisions in the system of local rule (Hailey 1957:55).

Meanwhile, in New Guinea, the practical value of anthropology and anthropologists in the administration of native peoples was being recognized. This was due largely to the insight of Hubert Murray (later Sir Hubert), Lieutenant-Governor of Papua, a humane and humanistic man with enormous empathy for the native. His anthropological solution to a smallpox threat has already been mentioned (pages 94–95). The idea of a government anthropologist was conceived by Murray in 1915, but because of World War I, it was not until 1921 that the first appointment could be made, that of Dr. W. M. Strong, Chief Medical Officer of the Territory, with many years' experience as a resident magistrate. Apparently Strong had had no formal anthropological training, and shortly thereafter W. E. Armstrong, a Cambridge graduate in anthropology who had already done field work in the Massim area of Papua, was appointed to assist him. When Armstrong resigned he was replaced by F. E. Williams, an Australian anthropologist, trained in that country and at Oxford, who a short time later succeeded Dr. Strong. Williams remained as Government Anthropologist in Papua until his death in 1943, a term of service in the same position undoubtedly longer than that of any other applied anthropologist (Chinnery 1933:161; Rosenstiel 1954).

About the same time, W. P. Chinnery, who had begun duties as a field officer in Papua in 1909, became interested in anthropology; in 1919–1921 he read anthropology at Cambridge. Returning to New Guinea, he undertook applied work related to but quite different from that found in the usual colonial administration setting: he was placed in charge of native labor at a copper mine near Port Moresby, a post he occupied for three years. This is probably the earliest use of an anthropologist by industry. During this period Chinnery studied the 1,000 men living and working in the mine, who were entirely separated from the influences of village life as well as from those of government officials. Unlike Williams, he did not study and make recommendations to others; he ran the show. "Now, divested of all Government authority, I had to organize, guide, and control a large number of natives differing in type, language and culture, and varying in social and economic development, through the many forms of activity present in a full running mining organization. . . . You can imagine the effect of the sudden and startling change of environment and ordered labour on recently controlled cannibals and headhunters and the extremely sensitive adjustments necessary to keep the balance between native employees and European supervisors" (Chinnery 1933:164–165). Chinnery felt that the company had a humane labor policy, an opinion substantiated by the absence of desertions during his term of duty. Agreement with management's aims and methods undoubtedly facilitated Chinnery in his work.

In 1924, Chinnery left the copper mine to accept the first post as Government Anthropologist in the Australian Mandated Territory of New Guinea, and in the same year A. R. Radcliffe-Brown was appointed professor of anthropology at the University of Sydney. Under Radcliffe-Brown, a program of training for administrative "cadets" was established in which Chinnery also participated: young men were posted to New Guinea for two years to learn the range of problems that confronted administrators, after which they returned to Sydney for a year's study of anthropology and other subjects bearing on field problems. Those who successfully completed this three year apprenticeship were appointed permanently to the administrative services. By 1933, fourteen cadets had gone through the rigorous training. Chinnery also carried out field investigations himself and encouraged other anthropologists to come to New Guinea to make the basic studies that government anthropologists often did not find time to do themselves (*ibid.*). Although his professional contributions were much more modest than those of his colleague and contemporary, F. E. Williams, Chinnery played a major role in the development of applied anthropology.

British Applied Anthropology in the Interwar Years. With the expansion of the scope of anthropology and the development of its research methods and theoretical bases, and with the deepening penetration of England into its African colonies following World War I, the idea of an institute to spur research in Africa and to make contemporary anthropological knowledge available to administrators gradually developed. Thus the International Institute of African Languages and Cultures was established in 1926 with headquarters in London. Lord Lugard, to whom credit goes for the idea of Indirect Rule, was named the first chairman of the executive board of the Institute, thereby emphasizing the anticipated ties between research and administration. The new organization, said Lord Lugard in the lead article of the first volume of *Africa*, the Institute's journal, would have a dual role. First, it was to be a coordinating agency, a central bureau and clearing house, to make the experiences of researchers in Africa available to all workers in that field. Second, although the encouragement and sponsoring of basic research would be central to the Institute's work, the Institute's distinctive characteristic was "that its aims will not be restricted exclusively to the field of scientific study, but will be directed also towards bringing about a closer association of scientific knowledge and research with practical affairs." Although the work of the Institute was to be based on "strictly scientific principles and carried out by scientific methods," at the same time it would "attempt to relate the results of research to the actual life of the African peoples, and to discover how the investigations undertaken by scientific workers may be made available for the solution of pressing questions that are the concern of all those who, as administrators, educators, health and welfare workers, or traders, are working for the good of Africa" (Lugard 1928: 1–2).

Although the Institute received a major initial grant from the Carnegie Foundation in the United States, and as its title suggests, is supported by European governments other than England, it has always been largely a British operation. Most articles in *Africa* appear in English (although French and German are also official languages of the journal), and most field work done under the auspices of the Institute has been carried out in (former) British colonies, even when the field workers were nationals of other countries. In addition to *Africa,* the Institute sponsors a monograph series which includes many of the most comprehensive and theoretically important of African ethnographies.

Unquestionably the Institute helped direct the attention of anthropologists to topics such as land tenure, customary law, wage labor, and the basic nature of contact between Europeans and African societies, which previously had not played a very large part in ethnographic investigations. At the same time, the immediate effect of Institute sponsored research on African administration was less than Lord Lugard had hoped for. The reason seems to have been the basic conflict found in a majority of applied contexts between the goals and values of anthropology and those of administration, particularly in mode of publication. Forde sums up the problem:

> . . . very often anthropological findings which should have been of considerable value in framing and implementing policy were not appreciated by administrators, since they were embodied in lengthy studies or specialist papers. While from a scientific point of view these represented a great advance in the functional analysis of native institutions, they often assumed a knowledge of and

primary interest in, theoretical problems, and the relevance of their results to the immediate and even long-term problems of administration was not always brought home (Forde 1953:850).

Richards, reviewing the first fifteen years of the Institute's program, speaks approvingly of the work of such people as S. F. Nadel, Meyer Fortes, Margaret Read, and Isaac Schapera. At the same time she is forced to conclude that "In spite of these hopeful beginnings it must however be admitted that the Institute's first objective 'to provide a closer association of scientific knowledge and research with practical affairs' has achieved only a very modest success." Field workers were not often steadily or consistently employed by governments, and at the outbreak of World War II only the Sudan, Gold Coast, and Union of South Africa had government anthropologists (Richards 1944:292).

Thus, although the immediate practical impact of the Institute was less than Lord Lugard and others had anticipated, the work it sponsored played a major role in the development of new ideas and in the growing utilization of anthropologists in action programs. In the early 1930's, the Bechuanaland Protectorate government employed the South African anthropologist Isaac Schapera to make a compilation of indigenous laws and customs for the guidance of officials, and subsequently to study the historical development of chieftainship as it related to European administration. (Schapera 1939:96–97). In the same period, the administrator A. M. Hutt and the anthropologist G. G. Brown carried out their unique experiment among the Hehe of Tanganyika, in which they attempted to find ways for the most efficient collaboration between representatives of the two fields (Brown and Hutt 1935).

Later in the same decade, in 1938, the Rhodes-Livingstone Institute (now the Institute of Social Research of the University of Zambia) was established, in what at that time was Northern Rhodesia, for the purpose of gathering information on tribal peoples to aid in administration as well as to contribute to the corpus of basic data on Rhodesian peoples. Although Institute anthropologists emphasized basic research, a number of papers dealing with practical problems of administration were published. While it is difficult to say how much credit is due the Institute, it is note-worthy that Northern Rhodesia was one of the best administered of British African dependencies, and that its independence was achieved with a minimum of friction and hard feeling.

Technological Development in British Africa. Although effi-cient and humane administration was generally seen as the rai-son d'être for applied anthropology in British Africa, some atten-tion was given to the cultural aspects of development. Mumford's 1929 analysis of the conflict between native need and British edu-cation policies is remarkable both for its time and for its insights. Mumford points out that although the Colonial Office's official policy on education for Africans was to adapt teaching to the mentality, aptitudes, occupations, and traditions of the people concerned, conserving as much as possible "all sound and healthy elements in the fabric of their social life," in fact practice diverged greatly from theory. "Excellent and efficient copies of British public schools, trade schools, and the like abound in Africa, but the writer knows of no schools definitely built on native tradition and custom. In the late nineteenth century an elementary educa-tion of an academic type was regarded as suitable for all classes, and presumably for all races. Early educationists in Africa there-fore modelled their schools on European traditions" (Mumford 1929:141). Mumford then describes several experimental schools in Tanganyika in which greater attention paid to indigenous forms and backgrounds resulted in more functional education. Unfortunately, in spite of this early insight, African education in British dependencies was modeled on English patterns until these countries achieved independence. In Northern Rhodesia in 1962, I found the traditional emphasis to be on "standards" and on aca-demic preparation of a type that would permit scholars to enter British universities, even though this was a goal to which only a fraction could aspire.

Also noteworthy in the field of colonial education was the work of the Colonial Department of the University of London Institute of Education (Read 1943, 1950, 1955). After World War II, in-

creasing support was given to problems of economic and social
development as well as of administration, and by 1952, about
twenty-five anthropologists had received Colonial Office assignments of from two to four years, to carry out investigations re-
quested or approved by colonial governments in fields such as the
improvement of cattle raising, conservation and control of soil
erosion, education, the teaching of hygiene, agricultural development, and urbanization and wage labor in cities and mines. Anthropological research and teaching was introduced or strengthened
through new units in local institutions, such as the East African
Institute of Social Research at Makerere College, Kamapala,
Uganda (opened in 1950), the West African Institute of Social
and Economic Research at University College, Ibadan, Nigeria
(also set up in 1950), and the Department of Social Studies at
University College at Accra, Ghana. Particularly important during these postwar years was the development in West Africa of
the principles of fundamental education, a movement now usually
known as community development (e.g., du Sautoy 1958).

In spite of these beginnings, the interest of Britain's applied anthropologists in the social aspects of technological development
has been relatively modest as compared to that of the Americans,
and books such as Margaret Read's *Culture, Health, and Disease*
(1966) are the exception rather than the rule. Looking at the record, one receives the strong impression that British anthropologists became disillusioned with applied work following World
War II, and that most of them failed to develop a new interest in
the use of their discipline in achieving directed change in the
fields in which American anthropologists work.

This loss of interest appears to stem from a growing disenchantment with the colonial policies of their government. Before World
War II, few if any British anthropologists working in Africa fore-
saw the rapid postwar dissolution of the empire. They assumed
that British rule would continue for many decades, and that
through education and experience, native peoples in each dependency would be brought gradually to the point of self-government — within the empire. They agreed basically with their gov-

ernment's policies and with the principle of Indirect Rule, and they felt that, as anthropologists, they were participating in plans and policies of which they approved.

But in the immediate postwar years, it became clear that the governments of many colonial dependencies, whatever Britain's official position, continued to look upon Africans as peoples who would need a long period of slow tutelage, and who would have to be taught a great deal about European culture and society before they could be trusted with home rule. Anthropologists increasingly felt that continued participation in administration and development meant that they were being used for ends with which they did not sympathize. As late as 1962, in Northern Rhodesia, I found government's view of the anthropologist's role to be that of the specialist who could tell how natives could be persuaded to do what the government felt was best for them.

In the first flush of enthusiasm for applied anthropology, Lucy Mair wrote in a 1935 article on "The Anthropologist's Approach to Native Education" that "It is because he claims that his science can interpret native society in a way which indicates what innovations from outside can be assimilated by it, and where a sound basis can be found for developments, that the anthropologist offers his services to the practical man." And concerning education, the anthropologist "can show where modern educational institutions cause unnecessary dislocation in the lives of the families whose children pass through them, and, from what he knows of the life that the adult native will have to lead, he can draw conclusions as to the type of education which will be of most real value to him" (Mair 1957:40).

Twenty years later, in "Applied Anthropology and Development Policies," the euphoria is gone: "The phrase 'social engineering,' which some of us used with confidence a generation ago, is now out of favour" (*ibid.*:10). And again, "The word [applied] recalls the confident 'social engineering' days in which it was born" (*ibid.*:11). And finally, in speaking of technical assistance teams, "Sometimes they turn to the anthropologist for the answer, particularly in America, where this kind of problem is new, and anthropologists *have not yet lost the confidence* that some of us in Britain once had" (*ibid.*:13 — emphasis added).

Whatever the reasons, American anthropologists, in the numbers and variety of tasks to which they turn their attentions, have taken over the lead, and the interest, which characterized England for several decades.

IN THE UNITED STATES

Until World War II the development of applied anthropology in America roughly paralleled that of Britain. The recognition that cultural differences presented special problems in the administration of dependent peoples, and that it was important to have information on such peoples, came early in both countries. Simultaneously, eminent authorities insisted upon the practical value of anthropology, but took no steps to demonstrate just how it could be made operational. The role of government anthropologist appeared in Britain rather earlier than in the United States, a fact presumably attributable to the vastly different sizes of the two colonial empires, and the numbers and varieties of dependent peoples. But, until World War II, applied activities in the two countries were roughly comparable, and only during and after the war, as we shall see, did notable differences develop.

Early American Applied Anthropology. A proto-applied anthropological period in the United States, such as that described by Reining for Britain, has not come to light, although it is quite possible that a study of slavery and abolition documents would reveal one. In this country the idea of the practical use of anthropology seems to have occurred first with respect to the native American Indian populations, our equivalent to dependent peoples in a colonial empire. In the second half of the nineteenth century, when it became apparent that the West would be settled effectively and quickly as a consequence of the expansion of a vast railway network, it was realized that the government would have to come to terms with the Indian tribes which still followed in significant degree their traditional ways, and which were not yet subject to the law of the country. Some white Americans thought the Indians would largely disappear, as they had in the East; others believed that in time they would come to resemble the white man in culture, successfully making the transition from savagery (as their state was then described) to civilization.

Congress' concern with the West, including its native peoples, is evidenced by its support of the exploration of the Colorado River in 1869 under the direction of Major John Wesley Powell. This work was continued in the second division of the Geographical and Geological Survey of the Territories, and finally in the Geographical and Geological Survey of the Rocky Mountain Region. The work of the Survey, under the direction of Major Powell, included a great deal of ethnographic investigation in the western states and territories and in Alaska. When, in 1879, this organization was consolidated with the United States Geological Survey, Congress authorized formation of the Bureau of Ethnology (shortly thereafter, "American" Ethnology), as a unit in the Smithsonian Institution, to carry on the anthropological research. Major Powell was the Bureau's first chief.

In the *First Annual Report* of the Bureau of Ethnology, Major Powell describes the ethnographic work of the Survey, which is to be carried on in the new organization, emphasizing its practical motivation: "In pursuing these ethnographic investigations it has been the endeavor as far as possible to produce results that would be of practical value in the administration of Indian affairs, and for this purpose especial attention has been paid to vital statistics, to the discovery of linguistic affinities, the progress made by the Indians toward civilization, and the causes and remedies for the inevitable conflict that arises from the spread of civilization over a region previously inhabited by savages" (Powell 1881:xi). Congress, it is clear, was not interested in supporting pure research; its intention was to further investigations that would aid in the taming of the West. Nevertheless, after this initial lip service to the principle, the publications of the Bureau were largely descriptive, and there is little evidence that they played any role in determining Indian policy. Even Major Powell does not return to the subject.

Nothing more is heard of applied anthropology in the United States until the anthropologist Daniel G. Brinton, in his presidential address to The American Association for the Advancement of Science, said that, in addition to its abstract side, anthropology "is also and preëminently an applied science, one the practicality and immediate pertinence of which to daily affairs render it utilitarian in the highest degree" (Brinton 1896:14). In what is perhaps the first specific use of the phrase, "applied anthropology," he continued, "Applied anthropology has for its aims to bring to bear on the improvement of the species, regarded on the one hand as groups, and on the other as individuals, the results obtained by ethnography, ethnology and psychology" (*ibid*.:14–15).

Six years later, Frank Russell, in his presidential address to the American Folklore Society, spoke in glowing terms of the utility of anthropology, pointing to its ability to broaden a person's mind and character, to develop his reasoning powers, and to equip a merchant, physician, or attorney with a practical knowledge of the motives of his clients and competitors. Quite correctly he noted its value to "aspirants for honors in the diplomatic service" where, among other things, a man learns the "characteristics of the particular people among whom his duties lead him" (Russell 1902:17). Then, warming to his subject, he continued: "For the legislator, anthropology must become a necessary preparation. America has problems whose solution calls for the widest knowledge of races and cultures. Such knowledge, free from political bias and hereditary prejudices, can best be gained by the study of the Science of Man. The list of these problems is a formidable one, including Philippine slavery, Mohammedan harems, Tagal insurrections, Spanish-American complications, coolie labor, the negro problem, the Indian question, not to mention the demands for legislation that shall regulate the immigration of Poles, Russians, Jews, Hungarians, and others" (*ibid*.:12–13). Fortunately, anthropology was not called upon to supply immediate answers to all these "problems."

In a far more perceptive vein, Walter Hough, commenting in 1907 on the then new policy of recruiting career foreign service

officers, urged special training for them with anthropology as the
basis, "since most of the misunderstandings and frictions between
alien peoples has been due to lack of knowledge concerning racial
habits, customs, and modes of thought" (Hough 1907:768–769).

A few years earlier, following the Spanish-American War of
1898, the United States had taken over the Philippine Islands.
Here, as with the American Indians of the West, government was
faced with the problem of administering diverse native peoples,
but with even less knowledge of their languages and cultures than
those of the Indians. Presumably modeling its activities on the
Bureau of American Ethnology, the Department of the Interior
established a Philippine Ethnological Survey which functioned
from 1906 to 1910, directed by the anthropologist Albert E. Jenks.
In spite of the Survey's ostensible purpose of supplying information
to the government about the peoples, cultures, and languages of the
islands to aid in administration, as with the Bureau of American
Ethnology, its monographs were of a traditional nature, to be
read largely by professional anthropologists (Kennard and
Macgregor 1953:832).

Jenks, however, had genuine applied interests, and some years
after his return to the University of Minnesota he instituted an
Americanization Training Course whose ". . . object is the training of Americanization leaders to hasten the assimilation of the
various peoples in America toward the highest common standards
and ideals of America practicable for each generation. The course
is founded on our anthropology courses which had already been
developed" (Jenks 1921a:248). Although this program aroused a
good deal of nonanthropological interest at the time, it had no apparent influence on the development of applied anthropology in
the United States. Jenks was also one of the first anthropologists
to propose research on Negro culture "to help our nation in the
solution of the Negro problem" (Jenks 1921b:154–156).

Edgar L. Hewett was thinking of the Philippine problem when,
in 1905, he wrote on anthropology and education in a manner so
modern that it is meaningful today. He speaks first of the "delight-
ful elasticity and inclusiveness of our several sciences" which per-

mit inclusion of the domains of psychology and sociology in an anthropological discussion. Then he criticizes the Bureau of Indian Affairs' educational policy, saying that "Unhappily, Americanization is often thought to be education" (Hewett 1905:9). In one of the earliest statements on cultural relativism, he notes that "A sound, commonplace aim to keep in view in educating Americans is *to make better Americans*; in educating Indians *to make better Indians*; in educating Filipinos *to make better Filipinos*; and it should especially be noted that when the term is applied to the process of improving any race or individual that is not formally praying to be absorbed into the citizenship of the United States, it in no sense implies *to Americanize*" (*ibid.*:2). Cautioning against repeating in the Philippines the Bureau of Indian Affairs' error of giving copies of American schools to Indians, he suggests that it is "premature and wasteful to establish there a public school system in advance of any considerable scientific knowledge of the Malay race. . . . There is really no cause for haste. It is hardly time to put the Filipinos to school to us. Let us go to school to them for a while. We can learn much from them that will be for their good and ours" (*ibid.*:14). For this definition of problem and philosophical stance, Hewett deserves to be called the first American applied anthropologist.

The First Applied Research in the United States. The first formal applied anthropological work in the United States began only in 1934, when two government offices — the Bureau of Indian Affairs of the Department of the Interior, and the Soil Conservation Service of the Department of Agriculture — initiated programs making extensive use of anthropologists. In that year, Congress passed the Indian Reorganization Act, a bill designed to extend the progressive social legislation of the New Deal (which began in 1933 when Franklin D. Roosevelt took office) to American Indians. Basically the bill was designed to restore to the Indians a great deal of the management of their own affairs, to attempt to check depletion of natural resources, and to build a viable economic structure for tribal life. In many ways its methods and goals were similar to Indirect Rule in Africa. Anthropologists were utilized in the Applied Anthropology Unit, directed for the first three years by the anthropologist Scudder Mekeel. In addition, Mekeel served as representative of and consultant to John Collier, Commissioner of Indian Affairs (1933–1945), under whose direction policies concerning Indians were drastically revised.

The anthropologists investigated such subjects as leadership and informal government patterns on reservations, and they made recommendations with respect to tribal charters and constitutions which were to be introduced. The anthropologists were "direct hire" employees of the Indian Service; that is, they were not consultants on loan from other organizations, but were tied directly to administration. In spite of this favorable circumstance — that the anthropologists had a formal line of communication to administration — and in spite of enthusiastic support from Commissioner Collier, the operation was by no means an unqualified success. One reason was that the Indian Service, moved by its own bureaucratic dynamic, and anxious to show results, pushed on with its work, so Indian constitutions were drafted and subjected to tribal vote, councils were elected, and charters were approved for tribal incorporation before research had been completed on existing social structures and degrees of acculturation. Another reason was that old-line bureaucrats, committed from their earliest days with the Indian Service to the previous "melting-pot" assimilation philosophy, were not in sympathy with the new aims (Mekeel 1944). In addition, the anthropologists tended to a more traditional view of research than the task called for. They did not fully appreciate the personal disorganization stemming from reservation life and from differing degrees of acculturation, and they were more interested in studying the surviving aboriginal leadership patterns and social structure than the new patterns and new social values emerging under reservation life (Kennard and Macgregor 1953:833).

The Soil Conservation Service teams, composed of anthropologists, sociologists, and economists, made socioeconomic surveys of the Navajo, and of Spanish-American and Anglo-American peoples in the Rio Grande Valley of New Mexico. Here, knowledge about the differential dependency of these peoples of greatly different cultural backgrounds on their land resources, and about the methods of exploitation used by each, proved to be useful in the planning of agricultural extension services and the implementation of soil conservation measures. The success of this initial work led to expanded use of social scientists in the Bureau of Agricultural Economics of the Department of Agriculture, and studies of varying types were made in many parts of the country. The wisdom and understanding of the government administrators in charge of these programs, and the nature of the research itself, led to what many have considered to be this country's happiest relationships between anthropologists and government administrators.

During the late 1930's, anthropologists were employed by an organization known as Technical Cooperation — Bureau of Indian Affairs of the Soil Conservation Service, whose purpose was to assess and plan for better utilization of natural resources on Indian reservations. Here again, as in the case of the Applied Anthropology Unit, the results were disappointing. The anthropologists found that, in spite of long contact with white culture, the Indians' significant patterns of social relationships and the prevailing values and attitudes underlying their motivations were still largely traditional. They insisted that the Indian administration would have to recognize this fact if real success was to be achieved in promoting economic and social change. Many of the administrators, however, even in the face of an official shift in Indian Bureau policy toward favoring such an approach, continued to believe that Indian conformity to prevailing white American patterns was the goal toward which they should work. This led them to believe that the anthropologists were sentimentally partisan to the Indians (which was to some extent true), and that they were unrealistically arguing for the preservation of the Indians' traditional way of life (Kennard and Macgregor 1953:833–834).

The most scientifically significant, and at one time practically promising, applied work on Indian problems was that done by the Indian Personality and Administration Research project, initiated and financed by the Office of Indian Affairs and carried out by the University of Chicago's Committee on Human Development and by the Society for Applied Anthropology. Like earlier social research on Indian problems, the project, which ran from 1941 to 1947, was designed to find ways to enable the Indian Service more effectively to meet Indian needs and enhance Indian welfare. Five tribes were studied, and a number of outstanding monographs and papers resulted. But the Indian Service, under new leadership, withdrew support in midstream, and the project was never completed (Thompson 1950, 1951).

In spite of the high quality of much of the applied anthropological research done among Indians since 1934, and in spite of the genuine interest of some administrators (including, of course, Commissioner Collier), Kelly writes in 1954 that "the Indian Service has not altered its procedures sufficiently so that anthropological findings are actually being applied or so that a professional anthropologist can work beyond the fringes of Indian Service problems" (Kelly 1954:709–710). As has so often been the case, the monolithic quality of an entrenched bureaucracy reluctant to change its values and views emerges as the principal reason for discontinuance of these early and highly promising programs.

Wartime Activities. World War II gave anthropologists an unprecedented opportunity to play a variety of applied roles in government. One dramatic example was their work in the Foreign Morale Division of the Office of War Information (pages 34–36). A Community Analysis Section of the War Relocation Authority used anthropologists to study and make recommendations on a series of problems associated with the forcible removal of more than 100,000 West Coast Japanese to detention centers east of the Sierras (e.g., Spicer 1952a, 1952b; Leighton 1945). One of the most important lessons learned from this experience, a lesson largely ignored in the early experiences of anthropologists in

the Bureau of Indian Affairs, was that "it is equally important
to study the assumptions, social organization, and behavior patterns of the administrative group, as well as of those administered,
since the two groups constitute an interaction continuum" (Kennard and Macgregor 1953:837).

Anthropologists also helped in training officers bound for administrative posts in occupied areas, prepared "survival hand-
books" telling downed flyers how to live off the land, and wrote a
series, "War Backgraund Information," short studies published
by the Smithsonian Institution on the peoples and cultures of the
war theaters.

The Institute of Social Anthropology of the Smithsonian Institution was a war-born program of a different type. Its establishment
in 1943 was one manifestation of an awakening interest in Latin
America and its problems, and of the recognition that growing industrialization and urbanization would be accompanied by a series of human and social problems. Anthropologists, sociologists,
cultural geographers, and linguists were assigned to four countries as visiting professors, to teach contemporary social science
and to participate with nationals of these countries in making
basic studies of rural communities of the type that might be expected to feel the growing impact of modernization. In spite of
the practical purpose implicit in the Institute's charter, the personnel conceived their function to be academic rather than applied. Although all were government employees, they taught and
did research much as if they had been professors in American universities. Personnel were not tied in with any United States or
host country action programs, and their work remained almost entirely unknown in such fields as public health and agriculture,
where it should have been of most use. A scientifically useful
monograph series was published, but the Institute, almost until its
demise in 1952, was in no way an applied venture. In 1951, however, its policies changed, as described in Chapter 1, and the store
of scientific capital acquired over the years proved to be of great
use in developmental programs, especially in public health (Foster 1967b).

The Society for Applied Anthropology. The Society for Applied Anthropology was formed in 1941, and the appearance of the first issue of its journal, *Applied Anthropology* (since 1949, *Human Organization*), in the fall of that year marked a turning point in applied social science in the United States. With a quarterly publication in which to present data and ideas that often seemed inappropriate to older and more traditional series, anthropologists and other social scientists now had a ready means of communication. From the very beginning, it was clear that the editors saw applied anthropology as a subject very different from and much broader than what previous opinion — either in Britain or in the United States — had held it to be. "*Applied Anthropology*," said the Editorial Statement in the first issue, "is a quarterly journal devoted to the solution of practical problems of human relations in the fields of business and political administration, psychiatry, social work and wherever else human relations play a part. It is based upon the premise that a science of human relations can only be developed if theories are tested in practice" (*Applied Anthropology* 1941:1[1]:1). The feature articles in this issue tell us a good deal about the state of applied anthropology in the United States at this time:

> Eliot D. Chapple, "Organization Problems in Industry"
> Froelich Rainey, "Native Economy and Survival in Arctic Alaska"
> William F. Whyte, "The Social Role of the Settlement House"
> Margaret Mead, "On Methods of Implementing a National Morale Program"
> F. L. W. Richardson, Jr., "Community Resettlement in a Depressed Coal Region"

In these articles there is no mention of administration or control of native or dependent peoples. Nor is there mention of the problem of technological change and new individual habits, except in the Alaska article, which deals with the introduction of reindeer. What *is* noteworthy is the critical importance of *role relationships* and the ways in which people interact with each other. This theme has continued to grow in importance in applied anthropology, and today, as we have seen, it is central to almost all such analysis. Three articles deal directly with what today is called *community development* and the basic principles it involves, especially the importance of identifying and working with local leaders. This again has been an important field for applied anthropologists. Margaret Mead, at least indirectly, sees *communication* to be a part of applied anthropology, but she uses the term in the rather specialized sense of the anthropologist writing so that "the working statesman" can understand what is meant. Overall, the amelioration of social and economic problems emerges as a major theme in the issue.

In reading early issues of *Applied Anthropology*, one is struck with the vision of a number of the authors. In 1942 Alice Joseph, M.D., in "Physician and Patient: Some Aspects of Interpersonal Relations Between Physicians and Patients, With Special Regard to the Relationship Between White Physicians and Indian Patients," gives attention not only to Indian customs and beliefs as they bear upon acceptance of modern medical services; she also stresses the physician's self-image, his prestige drive, and his forms of ego gratification as being critical elements in how he will perceive his role and evaluate his patients' behavior (Joseph 1942). This is also the first contemporary treatment of an intercultural situation to appear in the journal.

In the same issue, the physician-anthropologist Alexander Leighton, in "Training Social Scientists for Post-war Conditions," raises the question of a more formal applied social science, involving practical training as well as theoretical preparation. "The suggestion I wish to make is that universities and institutions interested in the education of social scientists might organize periods of practical training in collaboration with the Government or with private industries" (Leighton 1942:29). Regrettably, this suggestion has not been followed up.

International technical aid makes its appearance in 1943, when Charles Loomis, in "Applied Anthropology in Latin America," describes both the Food Production Mission of the Institute of Inter-American Affairs in Peru, and a rehabilitation project in Ecuador in which the anthropologist Kalervo Oberg participated in planning the program and appraising the results (Loomis 1943). The following issue has articles on increasing food production in Georgia and in Portuguese Angola, on community development in India and among Spanish Americans in New Mexico, and on improved agriculture on a Sioux Indian reservation in South Dakota; such articles might well appear in a contemporary issue.

The Society for Applied Anthropology also early expressed its willingness to serve as a contracting broker for interested clients. The earliest use of this service was a contract with the United States Department of Agriculture, whereby the sociologist Charles P. Loomis, one of the founders of the Society, spent six months at Tingo María, Peru, analyzing problems of introducing an agricultural extension service in a society which previously had lacked this type of service. His work led to practical suggestions about extension practice in a Latin American culture (Loomis 1943).

Administration in Micronesia. Early in World War II, it became clear that the United States would acquire the islands of Micronesia controlled by Japan subsequent to German defeat in World War I. Relatively little was known in this country about the islands and their peoples. In 1943, the United States Navy, which had initial administrative responsibility, contracted with Yale University to gather and process pertinent information. This work was directed by George P. Murdock. From 1946 to 1949, the Navy also operated a School of Naval Administration at Stanford University and at Monterey, to prepare naval officers for administrative posts in the newly acquired "Trust Territory." Felix Keesing served as assistant director of the school. Also in 1946, the National Research Council organized the Pacific Science Board, to promote research in the Pacific and to supply practical information to government and other organizations concerned with the Pacific area. With Navy support, the Coordinated Investigation of Micronesian Anthropology (CIMA) project was organized, and during the years of its existence (1947–1948) thirty-five anthropologists, four linguists, and three geographers made investigations, principally in the Marshalls, Carolines, and Marianas. A successor organization, the Scientific Investigation of Micronesia (SIM), expanded the range of scientific topics and continued to employ anthropologists, although fewer in number.

The initial objectives of Micronesian research were not oriented toward immediate administrative problems, but were intended to obtain basic data on contemporary peoples (Spoehr 1951). The Navy, however, found that its needs were not fully met by this approach, and beginning in 1948 it employed anthropological advisers to interpret the formal studies, to facilitate utilization of anthropological data in day to day operations, and to aid in long-range planning (Barnett 1956; Criswell 1958; Macgregor 1955:427–428).

When the Department of the Interior took over the administration of the Trust Territory in 1951, the posts of Navy anthropological advisors were continued. Provisions were made for a senior appointment with the title of Staff Anthropologist in the Political Affairs Department and for a District Anthropologist in each of the five administrative districts. The history of anthropology in Micronesia has been described by Homer Barnett, first Staff Anthropologist (1951–1953) in the new civil administration. Particularly noteworthy is the broad support given by the Navy to basic scientific, as opposed to operational, research, a vision regrettably not shown by any other operating branch of government. None of the CIMA reports, for example, were prepared on request, and most were only indirectly concerned with administrative problems. This freedom to select scientific topics was undoubtedly responsible for the eminence of the anthropologists who flocked to the Pacific; a list of their names reads like an anthropological *Who's Who*. Even during the final year of Navy control, when more attention was given to the practical utilization of a by now vast body of basic data, field anthropologists were permitted one-third of their time for research of their own choice, while the other two-thirds went to administrative and/or goal-oriented research (Barnett 1956:91). In the contemporary university setting, the anthropologist who manages to spend a third of his time on his own research considers himself a most fortunate individual.

Barnett describes the roles and responsibilities of anthropologists as they finally worked out. Anthropologists were direct hire members of local staffs who functioned as researchers rather than (in most cases) as administrative officers, a role that permitted them to serve as impartial intermediaries between administration and the Micronesians. Neither staff nor district anthropologists had executive status. As experts on Micronesian culture, they were expected to devise and recommend techniques to accomplish objectives set by administration, and to help administrators foresee possible consequences of particular courses of action. But the decision to institute specific action remained with administration, and not with anthropologists. "In short, they [anthropologists] are responsible for means, not ends" (*ibid.*:88). Government anthropologists, although in greatly reduced numbers, continue to this day to serve in the Pacific.

In 1946 the Department of State established a Foreign Service Institute in Washington to give training in language and culture to Foreign Service and other American personnel — especially technical specialists in our new foreign aid programs — to be stationed abroad. For a number of years, anthropologists and linguists played major roles as staff members of the Institute (Kennard and Macgregor 1953:838–839; Macgregor 1955:426).

Also in 1946, Congress passed an act permitting Indians to sue the government for all real and imagined wrongs arising out of past relationships between the two groups. Cash recompense for lost lands was the most important issue. An Indian Claims Commission was established to handle claims, and the Department of Justice was charged with defending the government. During the 1950's, the Department of Justice employed a staff anthropologist, and twenty or more anthropologists served as expert witnesses and consultants in individual cases. The law firms hired by Indians to press their claims also made extensive use of anthropologists to provide information on aboriginal habitats, on concepts of land ownership, and on tribal histories (Macgregor

1955:422–423). The significance to anthropology of the Indian Claims Cases has not been fully evaluated, but it is clear that it reflects on the anthropologist's hallowed view of himself as an objective and dispassionate scientist interested only in arriving at "the truth." Here, for the first time in history, anthropologists of equal competence and similar training, with access to the same historic and ethnographic documents, were opposed to each other in a competitive situation, each committed to his side and *determined to win*. The presumed impartiality and objectivity of the aloof scientist who merely "furnishes the facts" seemed severely compromised when diametrically opposed conclusions were presented, the particular variant of "truth" depending on the interests of the side to which the anthropologist was attached. Anthropologists tended to come to the "scientific" conclusions that supported the cases of the lawyers on their side and discredited the arguments advanced by opposing lawyers and anthropologists. Without fully realizing it, anthropologists had been caught up in a system whose fundamental premises are quite distinct from those of science: the "adversary" system of law which sets up a contest between opposing parties, the winner of which has demonstrated "truth." To many anthropologists, winning the contest became the primary goal. In some instances feelings became bitter between previously good friends; in private and to third persons they accused each other of perjury.

The first major United States government international technical aid program was that of the Institute of Inter-American Affairs, established in 1942 as the operating unit of the Office of the Coordinator of Inter-American Affairs, directed by Nelson Rockefeller. Although the initial rationale for the program was to ensure critical raw materials (such as rubber) for the American war effort, and to augment Latin American food production so that individual countries could meet their needs if sea lanes should be blocked, health and education projects were soon included in each country's program. It was recognized that a healthy, literate population would favor achieving narrow wartime goals, and would provide a strong base for growing democracy following the war. Several

American anthropologists and sociologists, including Charles Wagley, Kalervo Oberg, the late Allan Holmberg, and Charles Loomis, were employed by the Institute in these war efforts.

After the war the United States continued developmental programs in cooperation with the governments of most Latin American countries, and significant advances were made. Nevertheless, as experience accrued, it became clear that social and cultural obstacles to the introduction of improved practices in agriculture, health, education, and community development limited the achievements of technical specialists, and that social scientists — technicians in human relations — had a role to play. Illustrative of the early work of anthropologists on this type of problem is the 1951–1952 research on public health programs carried out by Institute of Social Anthropology personnel (briefly summarized in Chapter 1). By 1952 the Good Neighbor Policy of President Roosevelt, which had made possible the Institute of Social Anthropology, was at low ebb, and it became necessary to terminate the Institute. Four of its anthropologists, however, transferred to the Institute of Inter-American Affairs, and for several years, in Mexico, Colombia, Ecuador, Peru, Chile, and Brazil, they blocked out many of the kinds of applied tasks to which anthropologists have since directed their attention. Some of this pioneer research is described by Erasmus (1952, 1954), Kelly (1956, 1960), Oberg and Rios (1955), Simmons (1955), and Jenney and Simmons (1954).

Meanwhile, in 1950, the United States government established a formal technical aid program, global in scope, as a major arm to its foreign policy. This endeavor, popularly known as the Point Four Program, has been officially designated, in sequence, the Technical Cooperation Administration, the Foreign Operations Administration, the International Cooperation Administration and, since 1961, the Agency for International Development. A great many anthropologists have worked for it, their numbers rising or falling depending on annual budgets and on the presence or absence of social science interests among administrators. Toward the end of the decade of the 1950's, the Community Development Division of the Point Four Program, under the direction of Louis Miniclier, became the largest single employer of American anthropologists in overseas work and, although the level of operations is currently much reduced, anthropologists continue to work in this capacity in Africa and elsewhere. By now anthropologists, as direct hire employees who have made a career of government service, as members of Point Four university contract groups, and as consultants on loan from universities, have probably worked in every country in which the United States government has had a technical aid program.

FRANCE, BELGIUM, AND THE NETHERLANDS

Until recent years, France, Belgium, and the Netherlands were, like Britain, faced with colonial administration problems. In attempts to solve them, each country made use of anthropological knowledge and principles, although in no country were the relationships between professional anthropologists and administrators as close as in Britain. In France, colonial service personnel were trained at *l'Ecole Coloniale* in Paris, where they studied the languages, ethnography, customary law, and colonial history of the countries to which they were to be sent. In Belgium, Brussels was headquarters for an international body for the study of colonial problems, *l'Institut Colonial International*, which included an anthropological orientation in some of its work. Future Belgian colonial administrators were trained at the *Institut Universitaire des Territoires d'Outre-Mer* in Antwerp, where the curriculum included training in general anthropology, Congo ethnology, Congo languages, and African social and political organizations (Barnett 1956:8–9; Keesing 1945:377–378; Nicaise 1960:113).

For anthropologists, the experience of the Dutch in Indonesia is especially interesting. A curious situation existed in that archipelago: a rather healthy applied anthropology was practiced during the last century of Dutch control, with little or no participation on the part of anthropologists. As early as 1864, colonial officers in training studied ethnology, and subsequently the time spent on languages, ethnography, and native law became so great that Kennedy went so far as to say that almost all the colonial administration was composed of trained anthropologists (Kennedy 1943:188). Held's view is more tempered. He points out that in contrast to the other Indological (i.e., having to do with the former Dutch East Indies) sciences, ethnology dealt little in practical affairs (Held 1953:866). Like the British, the Dutch practiced Indirect Rule, but in an even more extreme form in which every effort was made to modify indigenous cultures as little as possible. To this end, the ancient customary law, *adat*, was thoroughly studied, and all native justice was based on the local forms of this system. But, as Held points out, this was not an achievement of anthropology; rather, Indonesian law receives the credit, not only in this field but also with respect to native land problems. "This discipline of Indonesian law never was, nor is it to be, confused with anthropology; nor is it so considered by Dutch scholars" (*ibid.*:867). Civil servants were considered to be Indologists rather than anthropologists, which Held considers to be the correct view since the influence of anthropology on Dutch colonial policy was always relatively slight (*ibid.*:867, fn.). Nevertheless, the recognition by the Dutch government of its need to know a great deal about native life in order to carry out its particular colonial policies has resulted in a vast body of what, in other countries, would be called ethnographic data. These data, of course, are found in the literature of legal, economic, and other fields rather more than in anthropological publications.

In very recent years, a formal applied anthropology has appeared in the Royal Institute of the Tropics, in Amsterdam. The work done by Institute personnel is thoroughly contemporary, concerned with the social aspects of change and modernization in the same fields that interest American anthropologists. For example, one of the very best analyses of the problems of introducing modern medicine in a primitive area — in this case, New Guinea — has come from this center (Van Amelsvoort 1964). For the past decade, Dutch anthropologists have been attached to CREFAL, UNESCO's community development training center at Pátzcuaro, Mexico, to teach and to carry out applied studies. The most thorough Dutch study to emerge from these assignments includes an analysis of problems of socioeconomic development in relation to indigenous culture in a Tarascan Indian village (Van Zantwijk 1967). Other Dutch anthropologists also have been interested in community development and native problems in America (e.g., Huizer 1964, in El Salvador; Heijmerink 1966, in Mexico).

OTHER COUNTRIES

In most of Latin America applied anthropology largely but not entirely takes the form of "Indianism" (Spanish *indigenismo*), manifest in programs established to help solve those problems of Indian groups which stem particularly from their geographical, linguistic, and cultural marginality to the mainstreams of national life. This concern with Indian populations appeared first in Mexico, where it was a logical outgrowth of the social goals of the Mexican Revolution. As early as the Second Panamerican Scientific Congress in Washington in 1915, the late Manuel Gamio, head of the Mexican delegation, urged the creation in each country with a sizable Indian population of an institute of "practical action," charged with studying aboriginal peoples "with the exclusive object of promoting their development and incorporating them into contemporary civilization" (Comas 1964:21). More than twenty-five years passed before action was taken on this suggestion. In 1941, the Inter-American Indian Institute was established, with headquarters in Mexico City, and Gamio served as its director from then until his death in 1960. Since its founding the Institute has published an excellent journal, *América Indígena,* and under its present director, the Mexican anthropologist Gonzalo Aguirre Beltrán, it is pushing a vigorous publishing program as well as promoting better anthropological teaching, research, and utilization of anthropological knowledge in Latin American countries. Subsequent to the founding of the Inter-American Institute, most Latin American countries with sizable Indian groups have established national institutes. That of Mexico, the largest and most active, was established in 1948 with the anthropologist Alfonso Caso as its director.

Action work based on anthropological knowledge and aimed at raising the levels of Indian life was not, however, neglected earlier in Mexico. During the early 1930's, Moisés Sáenz established rural Indian schools and sent "cultural missions" to many communities to teach new ways. His major work in this field was an eight-month experiment in 1932 in which, using "social anthropological" methods, he and his colleagues studied a cluster of Tarascan villages in the State of Michoacán and carried out action programs in the hope of starting these villages on the road to a more complete assimilation with national Mexican culture (Sáenz 1936). Unfortunately, as has so often been the case with similar attempts, little permanent change resulted from this intensive experiment. The cultural mission idea, however, continues to be a part of the Mexican educational system.

The Mexican National Indian Institute has carried out a huge program aimed at raising Indian levels of living by building roads, establishing health centers and schools, setting up community centers, improving agricultural and animal husbandry practices, and drawing Indians into community action through which they help plan their own futures. Development and training centers have been established in many parts of the country, and for years the Institute has been the largest employer of trained Mexican anthropologists. One of its early major projects, the Papaloapan Resettlement scheme, was described in Chapter 1.

Anthropologists also have headed national Indian institutes in such countries as Guatemala, Peru, and Bolivia, where programs similar to those of Mexico, although on a reduced scale commensurate with the size of populations, have been carried out. In 1956 the Guatemalan government sponsored a highly successful inter-American *Seminario de Integración Social* (Seminar on Social Integration) to consider problems of incorporating Indian populations into national cultures. The Seminar was given a permanent secretariat, which during subsequent years has published a great many volumes, originals and translations, dealing with the native peoples of Guatemala and their developmental problems.

Although indigenous peoples have received the bulk of the attention of anthropologists with applied interests in Latin America, other topics, especially health, have been fruitful subjects for investigation and action. For a number of years the Ministry of Health in Mexico employed anthropologists making studies of problems of resistance to new health services (e.g., García Manzanedo and Kelly 1955; Kelly and García Manzanedo 1956), and very interesting reports on the relationship between culture and health have also come from Colombia (e.g., Gutierrez de Pineda 1955).

Anthropologists have played an important role in community development in a great many countries. In the Philippines, the Community Development Research Council of the University of the Philippines has for some years pursued a vigorous research and action program in local development (e.g., Hollnsteiner 1963). India's vast community development program has made use of Indian and foreign anthropologists, the former in both administrative and research capacities and the latter as researchers and evaluators. Here the penetrating analyses of S. C. Dube stand out (Dube 1958). In Europe, Italy has paid more attention to formal community development than other countries, and, although anthropologists as such have played only a small role in this work, their principles and methods have been utilized. One experiment is described at length by Friedmann (1960).

INTERNATIONAL AGENCIES

The United Nations and its specialized agencies — particularly UNESCO — have made modest use of anthropologists, especially in community development. Shortly after World War II, the late Alfred Métraux supervised a pioneer fundamental education (the term preferred by UNESCO) project in Haiti (Métraux 1949), and continued as UNESCO staff anthropologist until his death in 1963. UNESCO also sent a technical assistance mission to Liberia in 1951–1952, headed by the anthropologist Joseph Jablow, to aid in educational planning in that country (Jablow 1954). In the early 1950's this agency established three regional training centers for Fundamental Education, in Thailand for Southeast Asia,

Egypt for the Arab world, and Mexico for Latin America. At least in the Mexican center, anthropologists have been used from time to time in teaching and research.

The Pan American Union sponsored community development training courses in Mexico, Guatemala, and Bolivia in the early 1960's, in all of which anthropologists played leading roles as directors, teachers, consultants, and supervisors of research. In Central America, INCAP (Instituto de Nutrición para Centro América y Panamá) has made good use of anthropologists in studying the cultural bases of diet and attitudes toward health and food (e.g., Adams 1953, Solien and Béhar 1966).

CONCLUSION

In view of the long and varied history of the use of anthropologists and anthropological methods in practical programs, and of the high hopes often held in the past for a flourishing applied anthropology, it is sad to report that the state of the field is less auspicious than one might expect. Fewer anthropologists are employed today in American international technical aid programs than at any time during the past fifteen years, and the same statement is probably true of the major international agencies. Perhaps the growing use of anthropologists (in the United States, at least) in schools of public health, medicine, education, and social welfare will more than offset this decline in the field of international development. If so, this strengthens the suggestion made in the preceding chapter that the "outside-insider," whose primary tie is with a university, but who enjoys longer leaves and closer association with action programs than is the rule at present, will be the mainstay of the applied field for a good many years to come. The combination of the stimuli and research opportunities offered by this type of relationship may well hold the key to the major development of applied anthropology which ultimately will occur.

works cited

Adams, Richard N.
　1953　"Notes on the Application of Anthropology." *Human Organization* 12(2):10–14
Anonymous
　1866　"Race in Legislation and Political Economy." *The Anthropological Review* 4:113–134.
　1963　"Waters of Affliction: 150 Million Cases." *World Health*, July-August, pp. 24–25
　1963–1964 "Statement on Ethics of the Society for Applied Anthropology." *Human Organization* 22:237
Applied Anthropology
　1941　Vol. 1, No. 1
Arensberg, Conrad M., and Arthur H. Niehoff
　1963　*Technical Cooperation and Cultural Reality.* Washington, D.C.: Department of State, Agency for International Development
Ashby, Eric
　1966　*Universities: British, Indian, African: a Study in the Ecology of Higher Education.* Cambridge: Harvard University Press
Barnett, H. G.
　1956　*Anthropology in Administration.* Evanston, Ill.: Row, Peterson

1965 "Laws of Socio-cultural Change." *International Journal of Comparative Sociology* 6:207–230

Batten, Thomas R.
1965 *The Human Factor in Community Work.* London: Oxford University Press

Beals, Alan R.
1962 *Gopalpur: a South Indian Village.* New York: Holt, Rinehart and Winston. Case Studies in Cultural Anthropology

Blau, Peter M.
1967 *Bureaucracy in Modern Society.* New York: Random House. Studies in Sociology

Brinton, Daniel G.
1896 "The Aims of Anthropology." *Proceedings of the American Association for the Advancement of Science* 44:1–17

Brown, G. Gordon, and A. McD. Bruce Hutt
1935 *Anthropology in Action: an Experiment in the Iringa District of the Iringa Province, Tanganyika Territory.* London: Oxford University Press

Chinnery, E. W. P.
1933 "Applied Anthropology in New Guinea." *Report of the Twenty-First Meeting of the Australian and New Zealand Association for the Advancement of Science,* pp. 163–175. Sydney, New South Wales

Comas, Juan
1964 *La Antropología Social Aplicada en México.* México, D. F.: Instituto Indigenista Interamericano, Serie: Antropología Social, I

Conant, James B.
1948 "The Role of Science in Our Unique Society." *Science* 107:77–83

Criswell, Joan H.
1958 "Anthropology and the Navy." In *Anthropology in the Armed Services: Research in Environment, Physique, and Social Organization* (Louis Dupree, ed.). University Park, Pa.: The Pennsylvania State University, Social Science Research Center, pp. 15–20 (Mimeo.)

Dart, Francis E., and Panna Lal Pradhan
1967 "Cross-cultural Teaching of Science." *Science* 155:649–656

Dube, S. C.
1956 "Cultural Factors in Rural Community Development." *The Journal of Asian Studies* 16:19–30
1958 *India's Changing Villages: Human Factors in Community Development.* London: Routledge and Kegan Paul

du Sautoy, Peter
1958 *Community Development in Ghana.* London: Oxford University Press

Eddison, R. T.
    1953   "Social Applications of Operational Research." *Impact of Science on Society* 4(2):61–82
Erasmus, Charles J.
    1952   "Agricultural Changes in Haiti: Patterns of Resistance and Acceptance." *Human Organization* 11(4):20–26
    1954   "An Anthropologist Views Technical Assistance." *The Scientific Monthly* 78:147–158
    1961   *Man Takes Control: Cultural Development and American Aid.* Minneapolis: University of Minnesota Press
Evans-Pritchard, E. E.
    1946   "Applied Anthropology." *Africa* 16:92–98
Feibleman, James K.
    1948   "A Set of Postulates and a Definition for Science." *Philosophy of Science* 15:36–38
    1966   *The Two-story World: Selected Writings of James K. Feibleman.* New York: Holt, Rinehart and Winston
Firth, Raymond
    1958   *Human Types.* New York: A Mentor Book
Flower, W. H.
    1884   "On the Aims and Prospects of the Study of Anthropology." *The Journal of the [Royal] Anthropological Institute* 13:488–501
Forde, Daryll
    1953   "Applied Anthropology in Government: British Africa." In *Anthropology Today* (A. L. Kroeber, Chairman), pp. 841–865. Chicago: The University of Chicago Press
Foster, George M.
    1953a "The Use of Anthropological Methods and Data in Planning and Operation." *Public Health Reports* 68:841–857
    1953b "Relationships Between Theoretical and Applied Anthropology: a Public Health Program Analysis." *Human Organization* 11(3):5–16
    1961   "Public Health and Behavioral Science: The Problems of Teamwork." *American Journal of Public Health* 51:1286–1291
    1962   *Traditional Cultures: and the Impact of Technological Change.* New York: Harper & Brothers
    1965   "Peasant Society and the Image of Limited Good." *American Anthropologist* 67:293–315
    1967a *Tzintzuntzan: Mexican Peasants in a Changing World.* Boston: Little, Brown
    1967b "The Institute of Social Anthropology of the Smithsonian Institution." *Anuario Indigenista* 27:173–192. México, D. F.: Instituto Indigenista Interamericano

Foster, George M., assisted by Gabriel Ospina
    1948   *Empire's Children: the People of Tzintzuntzan.* Smithsonian
            Institution, Institute of Social Anthropology Publication
            No. 6. México, D. F.: Imprenta Nuevo Mundo
Friedmann, Fredrick G.
    1960   *The Hoe and the Book: an Italian Experiment in Community
            Development.* Ithaca, N. Y.: Cornell University Press
García Manzanedo, Héctor, and Isabel Kelly
    1955   "Comentarios al Proyecto de la Campaña para la Eradicación
            del Paludismo en México." México, D.F.: Institute of Inter-
            American Affairs (Mimeo.)
Goodenough, Ward Hunt
    1963   *Cooperation in Change: an Anthropological Approach to
            Community Development.* New York: Russell Sage Founda-
            tion
Gouldner, Alvin W.
    1956   "Explorations in Applied Social Science." *Social Problems*
            3:169–181
Gutierrez de Pineda, Virginia
    1955   "Causas Culturales de la Mortalidad Infantil." *Revista Colom-
            biana de Antropología* 4:13–85. Bogotá: Instituto Colombiano
            de Antropología
Hailey, Lord
    1944   "The Role of Anthropology in Colonial Government." *Man*
            44(5):10–15
    1957   *An African Survey: Revised 1956.* London: Oxford University
            Press
Hauser, Philip M.
    1949   "Social Science and Social Engineering." *Philosophy of
            Science* 16:209–218
Heijmerink, Johannes J. M.
    1966   "La Colonización de un Grupo de Indígenas en la Mixteca
            Baja, Estado de Oaxaca, México." *América Indígena* 26:153–
            172
Held, G. Jan
    1953   "Applied Anthropology in Government: The Netherlands."
            In *Anthropology Today* (A. L. Kroeber, Chairman), pp. 866–
            879. Chicago: The University of Chicago Press
Herskovits, Melville J.
    1936   "Applied Anthropology and the American Anthropologists."
            Science 83:215–222
    1946   Review of M. F. Ashley-Montagu, *Man's Most Dangerous
            Myth: the Fallacy of Race. American Anthropologist* 48:267–
            268
    1948   *Man and His Works: the Science of Cultural Anthropology.*
            New York: Alfred A. Knopf

Hewett, Edgar L.
1905 "Ethnic Factors in Education." *American Anthropologist* 7:
1–16
Hollnsteiner, Mary R.
1963 *The Dynamics of Power in a Philippine Municipality.* Manila:
University of the Philippines, Community Development Research Council
Holmberg, Allan R.
1955 "Participant Intervention in the Field." *Human Organization*
14(1):23–26
Holmberg, Allan R., Henry F. Dobyns, Carlos Monge M., Mario C.
Vázquez, and Harold D. Lasswell
1962 "Community and Regional Development: the Joint Cornell-
Peru Experiment." *Human Organization* 21:107–124
Holmberg, Allan R., Mario C. Vázquez, Paul L. Doughty, J. Oscar
Alers, Henry F. Dobyns, and Harold D. Lasswell
1965 "The Vicos Case: Peasant Society in Transition." *The American Behavioral Scientist* 8(7):3–33 (Special Issue)
Hough, Walter
1907 "Anthropology in Education for the Foreign Service." *American Anthropologist* 9:768–770
Huizer, Gerrit
1964 "A Community Development Experience in a Central American Village: Some Reflections and Observations." *América
Indígena* 24:221–231
Jablow, Joseph
1954 "Some Aspects of Technical Assistance in Liberia." *Trans-
actions of the New York Academy of Sciences* Series II,
17:143–156
Jenks, Albert E.
1921a "The Relation of Anthropology to Americanization." *The
Scientific Monthly* 12:240–245
1921b "The Practical Value of Anthropology to Our Nation." *Science*
53:147–156
Jenney, E. Ross, and Ozzie G. Simmons
1954 "Human Relations and Technical Assistance in Public Health."
The Scientific Monthly 78:365–371
Joseph, Alice
1942 "Physician and Patient: Some Aspects of Inter-personal Relations Between Physicians and Patients, with Special Regard
to the Relationship Between White Physicians and Indian
Patients." *Applied Anthropology* 1(4):1–6
Keesing, Felix M.
1945 "Applied Anthropology in Colonial Administration." In *The
Science of Man in the World Crisis* (Ralph Linton, ed.),
pp. 373–398. New York: Columbia University Press

Kelly, Isabel
1956 "An Anthropological Approach to Midwifery Training in Mexico." *Journal of Tropical Pediatrics* 1:200–205
1960 *La Antropología, la Cultura y la Salud Pública.* Lima, Peru: Ministerio de Salud Pública y A.S., en cooperación con el "SCISP"

Kelly, Isabel, and Héctor García Manzanedo
1956 "Santiago Tuxtla, Veracruz: Culture and Health." México, D.F.: Institute of Inter-American Affairs (Mimeo.)

Kelly, William H.
1954 "Applied Anthropology in the Southwest." *American Anthropologist* 56:709–714

Kennard, Edward A. and Gordon Macgregor
1953 "Applied Anthropology in Government: United States." In *Anthropology Today* (A. L. Kroeber, Chairman), pp. 832–840. Chicago: The University of Chicago Press

Kennedy, Raymond
1943 "Acculturation and Administration in Indonesia." *American Anthropologist* 45:185–192

Lantis, Margaret
1945 "Applied Anthropology as a Public Service." *Applied Anthropology* 4(1):20–32

Leighton, Alexander H.
1942 "Training Social Scientists for Post-war Conditions." *Applied Anthropology* 1(4):25–30
1945 *The Governing of Men: General Principles and Recommendations Based on Experience at a Japanese Relocation Camp.* Princeton, N. J.: Princeton University Press
1946 " 'Applied' Research and 'Pure' Research." *American Anthropologist* 48:667–668
1949 *Human Relations in a Changing World: Observations on the Use of the Social Sciences.* New York: E. P. Dutton

Loomis, Charles P.
1943 "Applied Anthropology in Latin America." *Applied Anthropology* 2(2):33–35

Lugard, Sir F. D.
1928 "The International Institute of African Languages and Cultures." *Africa* 1:1–12

Luschinsky, Mildred Stroop
1963 "Problems of Culture Change in the Indian Village." *Human Organization* 22:66–74

McDermott, W., K. Deuschle, J. Adair, F. Fulmer, and B. Loughlin
1960 "Introducing Modern Medicine in a Navajo Community." *Science* 131:197–205; 280–287

Macgregor, Gordon
 1955   "Anthropology in Government: United States." In *Yearbook of Anthropology* (William L. Thomas, Jr., ed.), pp. 421–433. New York: Wenner-Gren Foundation for Anthropological Research

Mair, L. P.
 1957   *Studies in Applied Anthropology.* London School of Economics Monographs on Social Anthropology, No. 16. London: University of London, The Athlone Press.

Malinowski, Bronislaw
 1929   "Practical Anthropology." *Africa* 2:22–38

Marwick, Max
 1956   "The Continuance of Witchcraft Beliefs." *The Listener* 55:490–492

Mead, Margaret (ed.)
 1953   *Cultural Patterns and Technological Change.* UNESCO

Mekeel, Scudder
 1944   "An Appraisal of the Indian Reorganization Act." *American Anthropologist* 46:209–217

Métraux, Alfred
 1949   "Anthropology and the UNESCO Pilot-project of Marbial (Haiti)." *América Indígena* 9:183–194

Morison, Elting E.
 1950   "A Case Study of Innovation." *Engineering and Science Monthly* 13(7):5–11. Pasadena: California Institute of Technology

Mumford, W. Bryant
 1929   "Education and the Social Adjustment of the Primitive Peoples of Africa to European Culture." *Africa* 2:138–159

Murray, His Honour Mr. Justice
 1921   "Ethnology and Anthropology." *Report of the Fifteenth Meeting of the Australasian Association for the Advancement of Science,* pp. 161–180. Melbourne

Musgrove, F.
 1953   "Education and the Culture Concept." *Africa* 23:110–125

Myers, John L.
 1929   "The Science of Man in the Service of the State." *The Journal of the Royal Anthropological Institute* 59:19–52

Nadel, S. F.
 1951   *The Foundations of Social Anthropology.* Glencoe, Ill.: The Free Press
 1953   *Anthropology and Modern Life.* Canberra: The Australian National University. An inaugural lecture. Friday, July 10, 1953

Nicaise, Joseph
    1960   "Applied Anthropology in the Congo and Ruanda-Urundi."
            Human Organization 19:112–117
Oberg, Kalervo
    1954   "Culture Shock." *The Bobbs-Merrill Reprint Series in the
            Social Sciences*, No. A-329
Oberg, Kalervo, and José Arthur Rios
    1955   "A Community Improvement Project in Brazil." In *Health,
            Culture and Community* (Benjamin D. Paul, ed.), pp. 349–
            376. New York: Russell Sage Foundation
Oberg, Kalervo, assisted by Frank van Dijk
    1960   *The Fishermen of Surinam.* Parimaribo, Surinam: Surinam-
            American Technical Cooperative Service [A.I.D.]. (Mimeo.)
Opler, Morris E., and Rudra Datt Singh
    1952   "Economic, Political and Social Change in a Village of North
            Central India." *Human Organization* 11(2):5–12
Paul, Benjamin D. (ed.)
    1955   *Health, Culture and Community: Case Studies of Public Re-
            actions to Health Programs.* New York: Russell Sage Founda-
            tion
Philips, Jane
    1955   "The Hookworm Campaign in Ceylon." In *Hands Across
            Frontiers: Case Studies in Technical Cooperation* (Howard
            M. Teaf, Jr., and Peter G. Franck, eds.), pp. 265–305. Ithaca,
            N.Y.: Cornell University Press
Powell, J. W.
    1881   *First Annual Report of the Bureau of Ethnology to the Secre-
            tary of the Smithsonian Institution 1879–'80.* Washington,
            D.C.: Government Printing Office
Radcliffe-Brown, A. R.
    1931   "Applied Anthropology." *Report of the Twentieth Meeting
            of the Australian and New Zealand Association for the Ad-
            vancement of Science*, pp. 267–280. Brisbane, Queensland
Rapoport, Robert N.
    1963   "Social Anthropology and Mental Health." In *The Encyclo-
            pedia of Mental Health* (Albert Deutsch, ed.), pp. 1896–
            1906. New York: Franklin Watts
Rattray, R. S.
    1923   *Ashanti.* Oxford: At the Clarendon Press
Read, Margaret
    1943   "Notes on the Work of the Colonial Department, University
            of London Institute of Education." *Applied Anthropology*
            3(1):8–10
    1950   "Educational Problems in Non-autonomous Territories." In
            Principles and Methods of Colonial Administration. pp. 193–
            204. Colston Papers based on a symposium prepared by the
            Colston Research Society and the University of Bristol in
            April, 1950. London: Butterworths Scientific Publications

1955   *Education and Social Change in Tropical Areas.* London: Thomas Nelson

1966   *Culture, Health, and Disease: Social and Cultural Influences on Health Programmes in Developing Countries.* London: Tavistock Publications

Reining, Conrad

1962   "A Lost Period of Applied Anthropology." *American Anthropologist* 64:593–600

Richards, A. I.

1944   "Practical Anthropology in the Lifetime of the International African Institute." *Africa* 14:289–301

Ritter, Ulrich Peter

1967   "De Hacienda Semifeudal a Comunidad de Aldea: Vicos." *Economía y Agricultura* 3(9):56–69. Lima: Asociación Peruana de Economistas Agrícolas

Rosenstiel, Annette

1954   "Long-term Planning: Its Importance in the Effective Administration of Social Change." *Human Organization* 13(2):5–10

Russell, Frank

1902   "Know, Then, Thyself." *The Journal of American Folk-Lore* 15:1–13

Sáenz, Moisés

1936   *Carapan: Bosquejo de una Experiencia.* Lima, Peru: Librería e Imprenta Gil

Schapera, I.

1939   "Anthropology and the Native Problem." *South African Journal of Science* 36:89–103

Schoorl, J. W.

1967   "The Anthropologist in Government Service." In *Anthropologists in the Field* (D. G. Jongmans and P. C. W. Gutkind, eds.), pp. 170–192. Assen: Van Gorcum

Simmons, Ozzie G.

1955   "The Clinical Team in a Chilean Health Center." In *Health, Culture and Community* (Benjamin D. Paul, ed.), pp. 325–348. New York: Russell Sage Foundation

Smith, Edwin W.

1934   "Anthropology and the Practical Man." *The Journal of the Royal Anthropological Institute* 64:xiii–xxxvii

Snow, C. P.

1963   *The Two Cultures: and a Second Look.* New York: A Mentor Book

Solien de González, Nancie L. and Moisés Béhar

1966   "Child-rearing Practices, Nutrition and Health Status." In *Behavioral Science and Medical Education in Latin America*, pp. 77–96. *The Milbank Memorial Fund Quarterly* Vol. 44, No. 2, Part 2

Spicer, Edward H. (ed.)
  1952   *Human Problems in Technological Change.* New York: Russell Sage Foundation
Spicer, Edward H.
  1952a "Reluctant Cotton-pickers: Incentive to Work in a Japanese Relocation Center." In *Human Problems in Technological Change* (Edward H. Spicer, ed.), pp. 41–54. New York: Russell Sage Foundation
  1952b "Resistance to Freedom: Resettlement from the Japanese Relocation Centers During World War II." In *Human Problems in Technological Change* (Edward H. Spicer, ed.), pp. 245–260. New York: Russell Sage Foundation
Spindler, George D. (ed.)
  1963   *Education and Culture: Anthropological Approaches.* New York: Holt, Rinehart and Winston
Spoehr, Alexander
  1951   "Anthropology and the Trust Territory: a Summary of Recent Researches." *Clearinghouse Bulletin of Research in Human Organization* 1(2):1–3
Srinivas, M. N.
  1966   *Social Change in Modern India.* Berkeley and Los Angeles: University of California Press
Steubing, Carl M.
  1968   "Some Role Conflicts as Seen by a High School Teacher." *Human Organization* 27:41–44
Temple, Sir Richard C.
  1914   *Anthropology as a Practical Science.* London: G. Bell
Thompson, Laura
  1950   "Action Research Among American Indians." *The Scientific Monthly* 70:34–40
  1951   *Personality and Government: Findings and Recommendations of the Indian Administration Research.* México, D.F.: Ediciones del Instituto Indigenista Interamericano
Tuchman, Barbara W.
  1966   *The Proud Tower: a Portrait of the World Before the War 1890–1914.* New York: The Macmillan Company
Van Amelsvoort, V. F. P. M.
  1964   *Early Integration of Rural Health into a Primitive Society: a New Guinea Case Study in Medical Anthropology.* Amsterdam, Netherlands: Institute for Tropical Hygiene and Geographical Medicine, Department of the Royal Tropical Institute
Van Zantwijk, R. A. M.
  1967   *Servants of the Saints: the Social and Cultural Identity of a Tarascan Community in Mexico.* Assen: Van Gorcum

Villa Rojas, Alfonso
  1955 *Los Mazatecos y el Problema Indígena de la Cuenca del Papaloapan*. México, D.F.: Memorias del Instituto Nacional Indigenista, Vol. 7
Weiss, Robert S.
  1966 "Alternate Approaches in the Study of Complex Situations." *Human Organization* 25:198–206
Williams, F. E.
  1923 *The Vailala Madness and the Destruction of Native Ceremonies in the Gulf Division*. Port Moresby, Territory of Papua: Anthropology Report No. 4
  1934 "The Vailala Madness in Retrospect." In *Essays Presented to C. G. Seligman* (E. E. Evans-Pritchard, Raymond Firth, Bronislaw Malinowski, and Isaac Schapera, eds.), pp. 369–380. London: Kegan Paul, Trench, Trubner
Wilson, A. T. M.
  1960 "Change Processes: Some Samples and Comments from Commercial Marketing Practices and from Collaborative Social Research." Cuernavaca, Morelos, Mexico: Conference on Malnutrition and Food Habits, 9–19 September (Mimeo.)
  1962 "Notes on the Introduction and Promotion of Protein Rich Foods." Rome: PAG (WHO/FAO/UNICEF), Nutrition Document R. 10/Add. 51, March 1962 Meeting (Mimeo.)
Wilson, Godfrey
  1940 "Anthropology as a Public Service." *Africa* 13:43–61
Young, Donald R.
  1964 "Behavioral Science Application in the Professions." In *The Behavioral Sciences Today* (Bernard Berelson, ed.), pp. 222–233. New York: Harper Torchbooks

index

231